King of the C

and

The New Chines

CW00506596

King of the Children

CHEN KAIGE AND WAN ZHI

and

The New Chinese Cinema

an Introduction

TONY RAYNS

faber and faber

LONDON · BOSTON

First published in 1989
by Faber and Faber Limited
3 Queen Square London WC1N 3AU

Photoset by Wilmaset, Birkenhead, Wirral
Printed in Great Britain by
Richard Clay Ltd, Bungay, Suffolk
All rights reserved

British Library Cataloguing in Publication Data is available

ISBN 0-571-15448-4

CONTENTS

Chinese Vocabulary – an Introduction to King of the Children *and the New Chinese Cinema by Tony Rayns* 1

King of the Children 59
    Translator's Note 60
    Director's Notes 61
    Cast list 63
    Script 65

CHINESE VOCABULARY
an Introduction to King of the Children *and the New Chinese Cinema*

TONY RAYNS

Of all the Chinese arts reborn in the years since Mao's death in 1976, film has had the widest international impact. The world already knows that *Yellow Earth* launched a 'new wave' in 1984, and the old prejudice that Chinese movies were synonymous with Maoist dogma has been demolished. One reason why this has happened so quickly is that film is a far more 'cosmopolitan' medium than literature, theatre, painting or music; the world network of international film festivals (backed up by art-cinema distributors and TV buyers) minimizes cultural barriers and puts films into global circulation very efficiently. The other, more important reason is that the new Chinese films themselves have taken foreign critics and audiences by storm. Against all odds and expectations, China's younger film-makers have succeeded in reinventing and revitalizing their cinema. Their best films are not only superior to Chinese cinema of the last three decades but also richer, more deeply felt and more imaginative than most other films in international circulation. They have *earned* their place on cinema and television screens around the world.

It's tempting to put an exact date to the birth of the 'New Chinese Cinema': 12 April 1985. That was the evening when *Yellow Earth* played to a packed house in the Hong Kong Film Festival in the presence of its two main creators, director Chen Kaige and cinematographer Zhang Yimou. The screening was received with something like collective rapture, and the post-film discussion stretched long past its time limit. The occasion was doubly remarkable because the audience was predominantly Hong Kong Cantonese – precisely the audience with the lowest expectations of Mainland China and its culture, thanks to the endless stream of double-talk from Beijing about the future of the British colony. The Cantonese are notoriously poor speakers of *putonghua*, China's national language, but many of the

I

questioners that evening were so intent on speaking to Chen and Zhang in a common language that they set aside their linguistic embarrassment and plunged in regardless. One of the biggest rounds of applause was for the young man who took the audience microphone and stammered out not a question but a declaration of love to the two film-makers: 'I gave up hope in China years ago,' he said, 'but if a film like yours can be made in China, then there's hope for all of us.'

There were enough non-Chinese present that evening to ensure that news of this 'breakthrough' film quickly reached festival directors and distributors in other countries. The torrid enthusiasm of the Hong Kong audience was repeated when *Yellow Earth* had its western premières at the Edinburgh and Locarno festivals four months later. The film began winning international prizes, and the sales staff of the China Film Corporation found themselves with their first-ever palpable success. These reactions offered an interesting contrast to the 'official' response to the film in Beijing the year before. The Jeremiahs of the China Film Association denounced the film as 'incomprehensible' and accused it of gloating on the backwardness of China's peasant masses. The Film Corporation initially considered the film virtually unreleasable. That could well have been the last anyone heard of *Yellow Earth* were it not for its triumph in Hong Kong. That the Hong Kong audience was overwhelmingly Chinese meant that the Beijing authorities could not write off its excitement as a foreign aberration, which is why 12 April signalled a crucial turning-point in Chinese cinema. It was the night that Chinese cinema came of age, and its echoes have been heard around the world ever since.

But the birth-date of the New Cinema could equally plausibly be put back two decades to 7 May 1966, the day that Mao issued his fateful '7 May Directive', calling for graduates from China's urban schools to 're-educate' themselves by going to live and work with the rural peasant masses. This was in the early months of the Cultural Revolution, launched by Mao as his bid to regain power in the Communist hierarchy from his 'usurper' Liu Shaoqi. China's cities were in turmoil at the time, largely because Mao's political initiative had unwittingly provided an outlet for the unsuspected reserves of frustration and dissatisfaction felt particularly by the young generation, who took the opportunity to run wild. Few responded voluntarily to Mao's call to 'learn from the people' when he made it. By 1968, though, the directive was being ruthlessly enforced as a means of bringing the cities back under control. Hundreds of thousands – eventually, 20 million – were uprooted from their city homes and sent to labour in the fields, rice-paddies, quarries and snows of the remotest regions of the country. The élite among them – those with university degrees and white-collar jobs – began trickling back to the cities in the early 1970s, although many had died or permanently lost their health during their time in the countryside. The longer-term victims were the younger men and women whose secondary schooling had been curtailed by the outbreak of the Cultural Revolution. They had neither jobs to return to nor any real educational foundations to build on, and the authorities offered them no legal lifeline back to the cities. They were expected to spend the rest of their lives in the countryside.

In the jargon of 'Maospeak', these young people were dubbed *zhiqing*: literally, 'educated young people', often mistranslated as 'urban intellectuals'. But the term, a typical Communist neologism of the kind that clutters up almost all Mainland writing and speech these days, resists translation because it so specifically denotes a particular generation of young people at a particular moment in modern Chinese history. Rachel May has tried to deal with this problem by coining the English term 'urbling' for her forthcoming translation of Yu Luojin's novel *A Chinese Winter's Tale*, but until her coinage catches on it seems less misleading to leave the term in Chinese. Hence the use of *zhiqing* throughout this introduction and Bonnie McDougall's translation of the script that follows.

The directors of China's 'new wave' films were all *zhiqing*, and their experiences in China's most backward regions shaped their thoughts and their work in many ways. It is not by chance that so many of their films have centred on the *zhiqing* experience or found metaphors for the alienation and political disillusionment that they felt during and after their time in the countryside. Most of them managed to extricate themselves from their rural backwaters by joining the army or finding low-grade manual jobs in China's industries as they recovered from the depredations of the Cultural Revolution. Then their success

3

in winning places at the Beijing Film Academy, China's only film school, gave them the right to live in (or move back to) China's capital city. Being students at the Academy, however, also made them members of an élite group, charged with future responsibility for the course of Chinese cinema, and forced them to confront and think through their attitudes to the 'politicized' culture they had grown up with. In a real sense, these were children of Mao: born into the People's Republic, taught in Communist schools, victims of Mao's political machinations. Perhaps the ultimate 'author' behind the New Chinese Cinema should be considered Mao Zedong himself. Certainly there would have been no 'new wave' without the '7 May Directive'.

Most of the *zhiqing* had been ardent Red Guards in the early stages of the Cultural Revolution. They were in their early teens when their schools were closed down, and peer-group pressures forced almost all of them into the role of *jijifenzi*, 'political activists'. Historical and sociological accounts have rarely succeeded in evoking the sheer intensity of Red Guard fervour in the years 1966–8, and transparently phoney reconstructions like the one in Bernardo Bertolucci's *The Last Emperor* have added a further glaze of instant mythology to the period. The crucial fact to grasp is that it was a period of fanatically intense devotion to Mao, a period when the highest aspiration of every urban schoolchild was membership of the Communist Youth League. Whatever other frustrations and aggressions were being exorcized when the Red Guards fought pitched battles with each other, vandalized historical monuments, raided the homes of intellectuals and persecuted their former teachers and other authority figures, their primary motivation (whether sincere or strategic) was to present themselves as bastions of activism. If this literal worship of Mao seems far-fetched, remember that these were children born *after* the Communist victory of 1949 and carefully nurtured in Communist ideology from their first days in kindergarten; their only knowledge of the 'old society' came from the peasants and workers brought into their classrooms to testify to its horrors. Some, of course, had parents who had brought them up with a broader perspective on the changes in Chinese society, but they were precisely the children doomed to rejection by the Youth League because of their 'wrong' class background.

4

It takes a considerable effort of the imagination to picture this phase of teenage Mao-worship. But it's necessary to make it in order to get some inkling of the political disillusionment that these young people underwent when they were packed off to the rural communes. On the one hand, it was brought home to them in the most brutal way that they were expendable, that their personal aspirations to Communist glory were meaningless. On the other, they were brought face to face with economic and social realities that they had been shielded from in their urban classrooms. Here is Chen Kaige on the shock that he experienced:

> I had a rather privileged schooling at a select boys' school in Beijing. A lot of my classmates were the sons of Party leaders; one was Liu Shaoqi's son. Others were from relatively poor families; they had got there on the strength of good results in primary school. But all of us were brought up in a big dream, believing in the Party, in Chairman Mao and in China's wonderful, perfect future. We learned nothing about the country's political and economic realities. It was only when I was sent to the countryside that I found out how the peasants did mindless, back-breaking work and still didn't have enough to eat. I used to get very angry and say that our teacher had taught us nothing but bullshit. But I don't think he deliberately set out to lie to us. The teacher was just as much a victim of the situation as we were.

The *zhiqing* were immediately a burden to the peasant farmers they were foisted on. They were ill-equipped physically for manual labour and ill-prepared mentally for the rigours of life in the remote countryside. Furthermore, most of the host communes were already short of housing, food and material resources *before* the influx of newcomers, and the need to accommodate relatively unproductive extra bodies made things even harder. As the *zhiqing* were disabused of their idealism, so they were given a crash course in *realpolitik* by the news that filtered down from Beijing: the successive ups and downs in the career of Deng Xiaoping, the sudden death and disgrace of Lin Biao, who moved overnight from being Mao's designated successor and 'closest comrade-in-arms' to being a vile traitor,

5

and so on. The Party's chaotic mismanagement of the state and the endless rewritings of 'official' history generated a profound political cynicism, which finally led to the mass demonstration in Beijing's Tiananmen Square on 5 April 1976 – nominally a gathering in memory of Premier Zhou Enlai (who had died four months earlier) but in fact an open protest against Communist Party rule. The demonstration was violently suppressed by the authorities, but it none the less sowed the seeds of the 'democracy movement' that sprang up after Mao's death and the overthrow of the 'Gang of Four'.

The Beijing Film Academy, closed down by the Cultural Revolution in 1966, reopened in 1978 in premises built for – indeed, shared with – an agricultural college in Zhu Xin Zhuang, a village some thirty minutes' drive from the city proper. In this isolated, makeshift outpost, minimally equipped and under-financed, the school managed to offer courses in five departments: directing, scriptwriting, cinematography, design and acting. It had an initial intake of 153 students. Academy rules stipulated an age limit of twenty-two for new students, but the point was stretched for students admitted to the course in directing. It had to be: virtually all the applicants had been *zhiqing*, which meant that they had squandered what should have been their university years in the countryside, in the army or in factory jobs. Entrance to the Academy was by competitive examination; 'class background' was no longer a consideration. Some have suspected an element of *guanxi* – the age-old Chinese system of 'connections' – behind the offer of a place in the directing class to Chen Kaige, since his father is the veteran director Chen Huai'ai, but there is no doubt that he got in on his own merits; far from interceding on his behalf, his father actually *opposed* his application. There seems to have been a refreshing air of pragmatism around the Academy's administrative offices at the time. Zhang Yimou was originally refused a place in the cinematography class on the grounds that he was over the age limit, but his aggrieved appeal to the Ministry of Culture was enough to get the rule set aside and secure him the place that his exam result had earned.

The Film Academy (which has now moved to larger, custom-built premises next to Beijing Film Studio) offered its students the nearest thing possible to a 'liberal' training in the difficult

6

circumstances of 1978. In addition to their specialist classes and compulsory classes in Communist ideology and the history of the Chinese Communist Party, the students were taught aesthetics, film analysis, literary analysis, Chinese film history and world film history. Thanks to Deng Xiaoping's 'open door' policy (and the generosity of the cultural departments of various embassies in Beijing), they had access to a much wider range of international cinema than any previous generation of Academy students. Their dawning sense of the wider world was doubtless strengthened by the increasing visibility of foreigners in China; the trickle of foreign visitors in 1979 had swollen to a flood by the time they graduated in 1982.

Even more important, they were first-hand witnesses to the rise (and suppression) of the 'democracy movement' in 1978–9, hence readers of the unofficial 'new poetry' magazines that were privately produced and distributed in Beijing in the early months of 1979. Magazines like *Today!*, first known in English as *The Moment (Jintian)* and *The Spring of Peking (Beijing zhi Chun)* had links with political dissidents like Wei Jingsheng, but their editors and contributors were, in the main, less preoccupied with challenging the supremacy of the Communist Party than with dragging Chinese culture into the twentieth century. These *samizdat* magazines, which frequently cited their constitutional right to exist but which were printed and circulated outside state control, constituted the first public platform for the *zhiqing* generation. The poems they published – by new but pseudonymous voices like Bei Dao, Shu Ting, Shi Zhi and Ling Bing – used both traditional rhetoric and imagery and a new 'colloquial' tone of voice to articulate everything from political critiques to statements of personal alienation. The literary establishment denounced this poetry with the label 'Misty', accusing it of trading in obscurities and lacking clear-cut meanings. But the authors quickly became culture heroes in the eyes of their *zhiqing* contemporaries.

For several years after the crushing of the 'democracy movement', the *zhiqing* voice was effectively silenced in Chinese art. It had not been easy to write and print unofficial poetry magazines (supplies of paper and ink are controlled by the state, and printers are not allowed to take on unapproved work), but it is none the less easier to print a poem than to make a film, stage a play, perform a piece of music or exhibit a painting. It was not until the mid-1980s that the *zhiqing* voice began to reassert itself, most strikingly in China's 'new wave' films.

According to Chen Kaige, he and the 152 other students who entered the Film Academy in 1978 shared a profound contempt for the cinema they had grown up with. In fact, the Communist cinema of the 1950s and early 1960s had been surprisingly diverse in both its aims and its levels of achievement, despite the Party's attempt to impose a 'peasant aesthetic' on the film industry. (Cultural bureaucrats took their guidelines for state-approved art from Mao's *Talks on Literature and Art*, delivered in the caves of Yan'an in 1942, which closely followed Stalin's prescription for a didactic, propagandist art for and about 'the masses'.) The 1950s had seen a struggle in the film industry between Mao's 'Yan'an line' and the older, less dogmatic traditions of leftist art in China, a struggle closely related to the Party's need to bring cinema to the vast rural audience for the first time. The struggle was sparked by the Party's distrust of its long-time allies in the Shanghai film industry, who had worked before and after the Japanese occupation to make sophisticated progressive films designed to hasten a Communist victory. The Party turned against these film-makers in the 1950s, partly because they were urban intellectuals rather than peasants or soldiers, and partly because their films had been exclusively addressed to urban audiences. The first 'Yan'an line' films were made not in Shanghai but in studios captured from the Japanese in Changchun and newly founded in Beijing, and they were made by Party members trained in Yan'an rather than experienced film industry hands.

The richest achievements of the 1950s and 1960s – indeed, the only films now remembered from the period – sprang directly or indirectly from the older Shanghai traditions: adaptations from pre-war leftist literature, historical dramas, films that contrasted the new society with the old but undercut their obligatory affirmations of Communism with a palpable nostalgia for aspects of the vanished past. But it was inevitably the 'Yan'an line' that finally prevailed; those unable (or unwilling) to toe it were pitilessly crushed – first in the 'anti-Rightist' purge of 1957, which ended a number of important careers and caused several suicides, and then in the full-scale persecutions of the Cultural Revolution. The 'Gang of Four' all but wiped out the Chinese cinema as soon as they came to power. First, they erased its history: almost all pre-1965 movies were withdrawn, the Film Archive was closed down, and all industry veterans (especially those who had known Jiang Qing, Mao's third wife, during her early days as a Shanghai actress) were subjected to vicious and often violent attacks. Second, they halted production of feature films for four years. When production cautiously resumed, in 1970, it was only to make film versions of 'model revolutionary works' from the stage. By 1974, when these 'works' had been filmed to death, the studios were allowed to embark on a series of newly contrived agit-prop dramas, which represented the ultimate refinement of the 'Yan'an line': ultra-didactic plots, schematic narrative lines, naïvely 'typed' protagonists and antagonists.

The film industry had scarcely begun to recover from the horrors of the Cultural Revolution when the Film Academy reopened and admitted students of the *zhiqing* generation. Whatever memories of specific films the students brought with them from their childhood, it is clear that the Academy's course in Chinese film history offered them a unique opportunity to assess their cinematic heritage; they were shown not only films made under the Communist government but also films made before they were born. Several of them – including Chen Kaige, Zhang Yimou and Wu Ziniu – have told me that they found some of the 'classics' from the 1930s both surprising and interesting, but their reluctance to discuss them in any detail betrays a general impatience with the past and a desire to get on with the future, traits they share with their contemporaries in other 'developing' countries. And their contempt for the cinema of the 1950s and early 1960s, which is real and intense, has to be read through their general sense of political disillusionment, which leaves them indifferent to Communist campaigns and power struggles of the past. What could be more sterile and academic than sorting the wheat from the chaff in 1950s' cinema, when every single film made in that decade was dedicated to the service of a politics utterly discredited in their eyes?

As the *zhiqing* students moved towards their graduation in 1982, they had before them both cautionary and encouraging

9

examples of attempts to 'do different' in the film industry. There was the curious case of *The Corner Forsaken by Love* (*Bei Aiqing Yiwang de Jiaoluo*, 1981), directed by two army veterans (Li Yalin and Zhang Qi) at the small Emei Film Studio in Sichuan, which startled the entire film establishment by the naïve directness of its attack on Party mistakes of the past but never rose above the most primitive level of melodrama. There was the even more curious case of Xie Jin, a long-serving Party member at the Shanghai Film Studio, who had won respect over the years for putting an authorial stamp on various more or less banal propaganda subjects. Xie stirred up enormous controversy with *The Legend of Tianyun Mountain* (*Tianyunshan Chuanqi*, 1981), a bold melodrama about the unending persecution of an intellectual and the first Chinese movie in many years to feature a wholly unsympathetic Party official, but then immediately 'apologized' for the fuss by making *The Herdsman* (*Mumaren*, 1982), which deals with another miscarriage of political justice but drowns in sentimental patriotism and goes out of its way to avoid criticizing the Party.

The students found more positive pointers in a film directed by the head of their own directing class, Zheng Dongtian. *Neighbours* (*Linju*, 1982, nominally co-directed by another Academy teacher, Ms Xu Guming) is a film about the chronic housing problems in Beijing, anchored in scrupulous social-realist observation and underpinned with judicious touches of irony – notably in its sardonic depiction of a 'foreign friend'. It tackles a contemporary subject without apology or obfuscation, and has the clear merits of speaking plainly and meaning business. Its lessons were echoed and redoubled in a film made for the Xi'an Film Studio by the middle-aged director Wu Tianming, *The River Without Buoys* (*Meiyou Hangbiao de Heliu*, 1983). This was one of many films at the time founded on the proposition that 'ordinary people' were quietly opposed to the Cultural Revolution while it was in progress (a proposition some distance from the truth), but it had striking qualities that lifted it far above other films of its kind. For one thing, it offered amazingly unglamorized images of life in the Hunan countryside, complete with nude swimming in the river and farm-workers shitting in the fields; for another, it presented complex and sometimes self-contradictory characters whose conflicts were as much personal as political. Most arresting of all, it was the first Chinese movie since a banned comedy made in 1957 to end with a question rather than an affirmation.

On graduating from the Academy, the students were posted to film studios around the country, in most cases to work as assistants. Chen Kaige, for example, was assigned to Beijing Film Studio (where his father is also a contract director) and spent nearly two years there working as assistant to the middle-aged director Huang Jianzhong. On the face of it, the newcomers had little prospect of bringing their ideas for a 'new cinema' to fruition. China's oldest and most prestigious studios – those in Beijing, Shanghai and Changchun – are overstaffed to the point that it is virtually impossible for any of them to break even financially in any given year. All of them are assigned production quotas by the Film Bureau in Beijing, and the number of contract directors on their staffs far exceeds the number of movies they can produce. There is thus a 'pecking order' for first claim on the year's rations of film stock and production resources, and newcomers fresh out of the Film Academy could always expect to come bottom of the list. Fortunately for the graduates, though, the Government's devolution policies had brought into being a second tier of newer and smaller regional studios, far away from the country's main urban centres and thus *not* overcrowded with veteran directors or inundated with excess staff. Most of these regional studios were headed by bureaucrats with little or no previous film experience, who actually had difficulty in attracting competent and experienced directors from the bigger studios. Some of the 1982 graduates from the Academy's directing class were posted to regional studios, most significantly Wu Ziniu to Xiaoxiang Film Studio (in Changsha, provincial capital of Hunan) and Zhang Junzhao to Guangxi Film Studio (in the provincial capital Nanning). To their surprise, they found their way clear to begin directing almost immediately.

The first professional movie made by 1982 graduates was actually a children's film called *Red Elephant* (*Hong Xiang*, 1982), co-directed by Zhang Jianya, Xie Xiaojing and Tian Zhuangzhuang for the Children's Film Studio in Beijing. It was possibly not coincidental that the film was commissioned and financed by Tian Zhuangzhuang's mother, the former actress

Yu Lan, who now heads the studio. But this film (a fairy-tale set among the people of a minority nationality in South-west China) was a one-off project, since none of the three directors had been assigned to the studio. On completing the film, which has never been seen outside China, the team members dispersed to their allotted postings: Tian to Beijing, Zhang to Shanghai and Xie back to the Film Academy as a lecturer. Meanwhile their contemporary Wu Ziniu also found himself directing a children's film at the Xiaoxiang studio. *The Candidate* (*Houbu Duiyuan*, 1983) was an assigned project, ostensibly to be co-directed with Chen Lu, a director already on the studio staff. Co-direction credits are a relatively common feature of Chinese cinema; they usually indicate either that an untried film-maker is being supervised by someone more experienced or that a studio is trying to justify the presence of someone on its payroll by manufacturing spurious credits for them. In this particular case, Wu made the film without assistance or supervision and managed to turn a highly conventional moral tale (about a fourth-grade schoolboy who has to earn his place on the school

martial arts team by improving his course work) into a vivid evocation of the realities of an urban childhood. Wu insisted on using direct-sound recording – still a rarity in the Chinese film industry, which relies heavily on post-synchronization and dubbing – and drew admirably naturalistic performances from his cast of children and unknowns. The result had much the same spontaneity that the Hong Kong director Allen Fong achieved in his début feature *Father and Son* (*Fuzi Qing*, 1981), but it was sufficiently out of the ordinary in a Mainland context to win the film a prize as the best children's feature of its year.

The real 'breakthrough', however, was made by a group of Academy graduates at the Guangxi Film Studio. The studio had been founded in 1974, towards the end of the Cultural Revolution, but it had never succeeded in making any impact on the national scale. In 1983, when Zhang Junzhao (from the directing class), Zhang Yimou (cinematography) and He Qun (design) were posted there, they found the studio with new management but without any clear production policy. They persuaded the studio head to let them found a 'Youth Production Unit' (it was formally announced on 1 April 1983) and plunged straight into production of their first feature, an adaptation of a long, narrative poem by Guo Xiaochuan titled *The One and the Eight* (*Yige he Bage*), set in the anti-Japanese war. The central characters are nine chain-gang prisoners, one of them a wrongfully accused officer in the Communist army, who demand and get their freedom to join in the fight against the Japanese. The original poem focuses on the valour of the wronged officer; the film is more concerned with the latent honour of the other eight convicts. Both poem and film end on a note of excessive national pride, but the film has other qualities that more than outweigh its reflex jingoism. These qualities are primarily visual: its images are composed and lit unlike those of any previous Chinese movie.

Although there is no doubt that *The One and the Eight* was a genuine team effort, hindsight suggests that the dominant creative personality in the team was the cinematographer, Zhang Yimou, who already had ambitions to direct. The credited director Zhang Junzhao has gone on to make two sadly undistinguished movies with other collaborators – *Work Hard, China Team!* (*Jiayou! Zhongguodui*, 1985) and *The Loner* (*Gudu de Moushazhe*, 1987) – whereas Zhang Yimou has gone from strength to strength as a cameraman, actor and latterly director. The film's distinctive look was achieved through careful art direction and innovative cinematography. Zhang Yimou explains:

> We reacted against the bland, uniform lighting we'd seen in most Chinese films. A lot of the story is set in cells and darkened rooms, and we resolved to use nothing but natural light – sometimes nothing but a few rays of sunlight coming through a hole in the ceiling. That meant shooting on full aperture, on very fast film stock. What we wanted was the look of woodcuts: bold, decentred compositions, and a real sense of *chiaroscuro*. We ended up filming on location in Ningxia, where the landscape is harsh and monochromatic; other sites we looked at were too green. We put the actors in dark or ochre-coloured clothes, and we encouraged them to sunbathe as much as possible, to darken their skins.

The One and the Eight was passed by the heads of Guangxi Film Studio, but received with total dismay by the Film Bureau in Beijing. It was accused of promoting defeatism and of failing to respect the historical role of the Communist army in the anti-Japanese war. (One charge was that the film-makers were too young to know anything about the realities of the war – in effect, a coded attack on the film-makers for daring to attack the romantic myths fostered by their elders.) Seventy-odd changes were demanded, and the film was sent back to Guangxi for reshooting and redubbing. It sometimes happens in China that films are banned outright by the Film Bureau (or suppressed on the orders of the army or some other institution) and never heard of again. In this case, a decision was taken to 'salvage' the film by revising it, probably largely because the studio could not afford to lose the revenue from distribution; the fame and popularity of the source-poem may have been a consideration too. In these unhappy circumstances, the film-makers altered certain characterizations, lines of dialogue and parts of the storyline, but managed to retain the film's original 'look' intact. The revised version was given fairly wide distribution in China, but it remained banned from export until 1987.

Nothing in the film *directly* reflects the film-makers' experiences in the countryside as *zhiqing*, but nobody in China doubted that its assertive originality sprang from a set of attitudes and aspirations typical of the *zhiqing* generation. Only film-makers with *zhiqing* backgrounds would have wanted – or dared – to make a movie literally without precedent in Chinese cinema, a movie aggressively out of step with mainstream culture and centred (without inhibition or embarrassment) on the foul language and rough behaviour of convicts. In 1984, such a film's refusal to romanticize or glamorize its characters could only have come from members of the generation that had shattered the Confucian conformity of Chinese society when they ran amok as Red Guards.

The film's immediate impact in film circles was redoubled by its knock-on effects. Other regional studios were inspired to found 'Youth Production Units' of their own; the most notable was the one in the Pearl River Studio in Guangzhou, to which none of the 1982 graduates had been posted. Before long, even China's largest and most conservative studios were inviting their

youngest recruits to direct, although usually not granting them
their own choice of project. Meanwhile Zhang Yimou and He
Qun invited their classmate Chen Kaige to join them in
Guangxi, a move that resulted in the making of *Yellow Earth*.
By the end of 1984, the *zhiqing* film-makers had drawn enough
attention to themselves to earn a nickname in the press. Chinese
film critics began referring to them as 'The Fifth Generation' of
Chinese directors. Despite murmurs of disapproval from the
Film Bureau, the label quickly stuck.

No one seems fully clear how the nickname was arrived at.
Some take it to mean that the film-makers were the fifth distinct
group to graduate from the Film Academy, which has a periodic
rather than an annual intake. But simple mathematics makes
that explanation unlikely: the Academy was founded in 1956,
closed between 1966 and 1978, and offers its students four-year
courses. Others take a larger view of Chinese film history,
seeing the 1920s pioneers as 'The First Generation' and so on,
thereby defining the Class of '82 as a sufficiently autonomous
group to warrant being classed as a new 'generation'. Whatever,
the nickname's underlying significance is that it implies some
kind of new beginning and stresses the distance that separates
the young directors from their 'Fourth Generation'
predecessors. Calling them 'The Fifth Generation' is a
characteristically Chinese way of saying that they represent a
'new wave'. Accordingly, the term was soon stretched to include
several directors who had not, in fact, attended the Academy
between 1978 and 1982 but whose work aligned itself with
'Fifth Generation' innovations. These included the Xi'an
director Huang Jianxin, who attended only a two-year intensive
course at the Academy after the Class of '82 had graduated, and
the southerner Zhang Zeming, who twice tried for a place in the
Academy and twice failed to win one.

There were twenty-seven students in the 1978–82 directing
class (eight of them women), only a few of whom have gone on
to earn the 'Fifth Generation' tag. Some have still not found the
opportunity to direct features; others have directed nothing but
more or less mediocre studio assignments. To date, a hard core
of seven youngish directors (all in their mid-thirties, five of
them Academy graduates) have signed the most distinguished
films of the 'new wave'. It is their films that have won a new

international audience for Chinese cinema in the years since 1985; it is noticeable (and somewhat embarrassing for the Chinese authorities) that hardly any films made by Third- or Fourth-generation directors have been able to benefit from the escalating interest in Chinese cinema overseas. However, very few of the 'Fifth Generation' films have proved popular with domestic Chinese audiences, and the gap between acclaim overseas and commercial failure at home has put a set of economic and ideological problems in the path of the 'new wave'. Before sketching the careers of the seven leading directors, it's necessary to outline the range and significance of these problems.

The Chinese film industry has lost nearly one-third of its domestic audience in the years since Deng Xiaoping came to power. This still leaves it with an annual attendance of over 21 billion (i.e., approximately twenty-one cinema visits per capita per annum), but the decline has been precipitous and alarming. In the same period, the level of production has roughly trebled: 45 features were completed in 1978 (when the industry was struggling to rally from the depredations of the Cultural Revolution), as against 142 in 1987. (Output actually peaked in 1984, when 143 features were completed.) The inevitable corollary of these statistics is that more Chinese films are losing money than ever before, but the Byzantine intricacies of the country's production and distribution systems make it impossible to reduce the issue to a simple profit-and-loss account. The Film Bureau (originally under the aegis of the Ministry of Culture; since 1986 under a newly created Ministry of Radio, Film and Television) continues to set production levels for China's sixteen main film studios, but responsibility for the actual choice of projects has devolved to the individual studio heads and the requirement to produce a certain number of 'national policy' films has been gradually phased out. Domestic distribution remains a monopoly of the China Film Corporation, based in Beijing and with branch offices throughout the country, in every province, autonomous region and major city. The Film Corporation is also responsible for buying and distributing foreign movies, while its import/export department also handles all overseas sales of Chinese movies.

The complicated rules governing the relationships between

the Film Bureau, the producers and the distributors have been in a state of flux ever since the industry's economic problems became too serious to ignore. Under the old system, the studios sold prints of their productions outright to the Film Corporation for a flat fee, and so studio profits (if any) would depend on the volume of prints ordered by the Corporation. The first two studios to challenge this system were those in Shanghai and Xi'an, which in 1986 negotiated deals with the Corporation to stop selling prints outright and instead share in box-office receipts. Neither studio was happy with the immediate results of this change. Shanghai suddenly found its production slate out of step with audience tastes, so that its revenues fell well below its projected earnings. Xi'an, on the other hand, produced a number of big hits but found itself with a severe cash-flow problem, because box-office revenue came in so much more slowly than cash from the previous sale of prints. Meanwhile the Corporation made some new calculations of its own and came to the conclusion that a film needs to pass 30 million admissions in China to show a profit. The figure is high because ticket prices are still pegged artificially low, and there is some doubt that remote rural audiences ever pay at all for the films they see. Zhao Han'gao, head of the Corporation's domestic distribution department, says that he lost money on 108 of the 142 feature films released in 1987.

The Film Corporation is currently looking into ways of divesting itself of its automatic monopoly in film distribution, along with its statutory obligation to handle all films passed by the Film Bureau. A symposium on Strategic Planning for the Film Industry (held in Beijing in June 1988) relaxed some of the controls on the Film Corporation, allowing it to increase ticket prices in some of its newer and more comfortable urban cinemas, but failed to produce ways of alleviating the financial problems faced by the studios. All but four of China's studios have opted for the continuing security of guaranteed Film Corporation distribution, and for the old system of flat fees for the outright sale of prints.

The studios face two daunting problems. First, all but the newest and smallest are obliged to retain over-large and under-productive work-forces and all have to pay very high taxes on profits to the state; these factors make it virtually impossible for the studios to break even in any given year. Second, in common with producers in the capitalist world, they have no easy way of judging what will and will not appeal to their prospective audience. The 'outright sale' system provides the more nervous studios with a bottom-line guarantee of *some* income, even if a film is inept or totally unappealing to the mass audience. A studio could expect to sell some 200 prints of an average title, rising to over 400 prints of an exceptional success. But a minority-interest film still risks running foul of this system, because 'success' rests solely on the judgement of the Film Corporation's branch managers. In 1985, for instance, nearly all branches of the Corporation declined to buy copies of Tian Zhuangzhuang's *On the Hunting Ground* (*Liechang Zhasa*), with the result that the Inner Mongolia Film Studio sold only four prints and had to write off almost the entire cost of the production. Most studios have responded to this second problem by rushing slates of down-market 'entertainment' films into production: crime and murder thrillers, martial arts movies and lurid melodramas. Many of these are clumsily copied from western and Hong Kong models.

The one studio head who has not caved in to all the economic pressures is Wu Tianming in Xi'an, already noted as the director of *The River Without Buoys*. He was elected studio head by the work-force at the end of 1983, and has since tried to keep up his own career as an innovative director while tackling the malaises of the studio's structure, administration methods and production policies. Xi'an is a medium-sized studio by Chinese standards, founded in 1956 and currently with a work-force of some 1,400 personnel. Its annual production quota is ten features, sometimes stretched to eleven by careful housekeeping. The studio was in extremely poor shape when Wu took over: staff morale was low, hardly any productions were showing a profit, and Xi'an films regularly turned up amongst the year's lowest-grossing titles. Using the success of his own *River Without Buoys* as an example, Wu tried to galvanize the studio staff into a more concerted frame of mind and began dividing his production slate between 'commercial' films (*shangye pian*) and 'art' films (*yishu pian*) or 'exploratory' films (*tansuo pian*). His rationale runs like this:

An enterprise is like a person: it needs money to survive.
Regular income. You have to go out to earn money,
otherwise you starve. But if you work *only* for money,
without any sense of your prestige, then your 'face' is not
bright. We make entertainment films partly to satisfy a
social need. There are different audience levels, and
entertainment films are for the general audience. They also
earn us the money to keep the studio going. But
entertainment films alone aren't enough. Chinese cinema
has to develop, and so artistic films are needed too: films
that break new ground and push film-language forward.
Films like that can have a big impact at home and abroad,
even if they are not big commercial successes. They
represent the studio's peak achievements in terms of art
and technique, and we make them for the sake of 'face'.
My policies spring from my need for both money *and*
'face'. Earning money without 'face' means nothing to the
studio. Winning 'face' but no money means the death of
the studio. And if the studio died, we'd have no 'face' at
all . . .

Wu's efforts have made Xi'an the most important studio in China, and have made him personally a figurehead of the campaign to reform China's economy and industries, as championed by Deng Xiaoping and his current protégé Premier Zhao Ziyang. Wu has skilfully produced both huge commercial hits and films capable of winning prizes in international competitions. But although he has moved the studio from the bottom to the top of the film industry's 'league table' and has tried to devolve financial responsibility for individual films to production groups within the studio, he has not succeeded in pulling the studio out of the red. The ten films he produced in 1987 grossed some 4 million *yuan* at the Chinese box-office, of which the studio's share was only 1.35 million. Wu calculates that the studio, with its present staffing levels, needs an annual income of 4 million *yuan* to break even, and notes that it is already carrying a bank debt of some 14 million. Not surprisingly, his current priority is to quit his post and set up in business as an independent producer/director. But his only hope of achieving this is to move to one of China's 'special economic zones', and even then he would still have to solve the problem of generating enough income from domestic distribution.

Part of Wu's importance is that his policies and strategies have exposed the fundamental impossibility of running a Chinese film studio profitably under the current economic rules and employment laws. Every other studio head is in the same plight, but Wu has been the most articulate and outspoken in bringing the problems to public attention. At the same time, his proven ability to offset his losses on 'art films' like *Horse Thief* and *King of the Children* by also producing massively popular genre films has provoked jealousy and a measure of resentment amongst his peers in China's larger and notionally more prestigious studios. Wu's successes with films like Li Yundong's *Legend of the Dowager Empress's Tomb* (*Cixi Mu Zhenbao Chuanqi*, 1985/86, a two-part saga of imperial grave-robbing and retribution, featuring a caricatured Chiang Kai-Shek) and Zhou Xiaowen and Shi Chenfeng's *The Last Frenzy* (*Zuihou de Fengkuang*, 1988, a surprisingly slick Chinese variation on *Dirty Harry*) have undoubtedly been galling to rival studio heads, who generally lack the courage and conviction to back such unashamedly gutsy entertainments. But it is Wu's loudly

advertised commitment to young directors that has done most to consolidate his notoriety in film circles. He prides himself on running a studio that is not top-heavy with managers and 'political advisers', observing that this makes it much easier for younger staff to exercise their talents and distinguish themselves. He likes to cite an old Chinese proverb: 'No tiger in the mountains, so the monkey can become king.'

Wu himself (born near Xi'an in 1939) first came to the studio in 1960, as a young actor. He began directing in 1979, at the age of forty, after attending one of the Film Academy's short intensive courses for students already on a studio payroll. The first two films he signed were co-directed with his friend and contemporary Teng Wenji: *Reverberations of Life* (*Shenghuo de Chanyin*, 1979), a Cultural Revolution melodrama about a musician's defiance of a 'Gang of Four' apparatchik, and *Kith and Kin* (*Quinyuan*, 1980), an absurd 'national policy' movie about the reunion of relatives divided by the Taiwan Strait. His first solo film, *The River Without Buoys*, was also his first serious and personal project; making it involved persuading the author Ye Weilin to retrieve the rights to his original short-story from Beijing Film Studio so that they could be reassigned to Wu instead. On becoming studio head, he immediately resolved to rejuvenate the studio by giving opportunities to young directors. He told me in the early months of 1984 that he was determined to let directors start working for him while they were younger than he had been when he started directing himself, and that he didn't see why anyone should be forced to start their careers on time-wasting nonsense like the two films that he had co-directed. It was hard to believe him at the time, but he proved entirely true to his words.

To start with, Wu Tianming tried to transform Xi'an Film Studio by making better use of the talents already under contract. He and his former co-director Teng Wenji both made serious and controversial films for the studio in 1984. Teng's was *At the Beach* (*Haitan*), an all-but-plotless sketch of a fishing village focused on the tensions attending its 'modernization'. Wu's was *Life* (*Rensheng*), a two-part film about a young rural intellectual whose emotional relationships are closely tied to his job prospects; Wu anchored the schematic storyline in small-town and village settings that he knew from his own upbringing in rural Shaanxi Province, and managed to make some forthright comments about the arbitrariness of the Party's commitment to reform. Both films ran into trouble in the first campaign against 'spiritual pollution' and neither has been much seen outside China, but both effectively signalled the new spirit in force in Xi'an. Wu did not find time to direct again himself until he shot *Old Well* (*Lao Jing*) at the end of 1986, but he honoured his plan to let other studio staff make more ambitious films. The forty-five-year-old director Yan Xueshu, whose filmography to date looked much like Wu's own, was encouraged to make *In the Wild Mountains* (*Ye Shan*, 1985), a lively tragicomedy about two mismatched couples in the Shaanxi countryside. The forty-four-year-old art director Zhang Zi'en was allowed to turn director to make *The Quiet Little Li River* (*Momo de Xiao Lihe*, 1985), a tense Civil War drama set in another realistically evoked Shaanxi village. While films like these were being made, Wu sent the studio's most promising young assistant director, Huang Jianxin, to attend a two-year intensive course in directing at the Film Academy.

By the end of 1985, when it was clear that Wu Tianming's policies were producing both artistic and commercial successes for the first time in the studio's history, Wu turned his attention to the 'Fifth Generation' directors whose films were already attracting as much attention in film circles as the recent Xi'an productions. He had talks with Chen Kaige, Tian Zhuangzhuang, Zhang Yimou and Wu Ziniu, and invited all of them to join him in Xi'an to work on innovative *tansuo pian*. The first to respond was Tian Zhuangzhuang, who spent much of 1986 in Tibet, Gansu and Qinghai shooting the Buddhist fable *Horse Thief* for the studio. Zhang Yimou agreed to work as cinematographer on Wu's own next project, *Old Well*, on condition that he be allowed to direct a film himself afterwards. And Chen Kaige (at the time, stuck in a stalemate over the final cut of *The Big Parade*) gratefully seized the opportunity to begin planning *King of the Children*. Wu Ziniu also began developing a project for Wu Tianming, but the recent banning of his film *The Dove Tree* obliged him to make another movie for the Xiaoxiang Film Studio first, in the hope of offsetting the financial losses caused by the ban. Well aware that he was courting further controversy by working with these film-makers, Wu Tianming formulated an ingenious rationale to justify most of the resulting projects: he announced that the studio would specialize in producing 'westerns', a highly elastic term meaning films set in any of China's western provinces and autonomous regions, from Yunnan in the South to Xinjiang in the North. (Xi'an itself lies in China's Mid-West, in the same province as the old Communist base Yan'an). Wu's argument ran that studios like those in Shanghai and Beijing were best equipped to deal with urban subjects, while a smaller studio like the one in Xi'an was best placed to tackle close-to-home rural subjects. Some of the resulting films (like Zhang Yimou's *Red Sorghum*) were not, in fact, set in western China, but the rationale served its purpose by deflecting attention from the real reason for the young directors' predilection for rural subjects: their own pasts in the countryside as *zhiqing*.

The primary problem faced by the directors of China's 'New

Cinema' is that their films are better known abroad than at home, thanks to the vagaries of the intransigent distribution system, which still fails to target its releases at specific sectors of the audience. This problem was compounded in 1987 by the reintroduction of ideological questions about the validity of the 'New Cinema'. Wu Yigong, the financially beleaguered head of Shanghai Film Studio, dragged politics back into the arena by accusing the 'Fifth Generation' directors of failing to 'serve the people' because they made films beyond the comprehension of the mass audience. The attack provided ammunition for the Politburo ideologues who saw innovations in film form as evidence of 'bourgeois liberalism'. Shamefully, this line of criticism was endorsed by veteran cadres in the Film Association (like Xia Yan, one-time head of the Party's 'underground' group in the old Shanghai film industry), who evidently forgot that they were once brave young innovators themselves in the 1930s. The antique Stalinist debates about 'mass culture' were quieted – at least temporarily – by the prizes won by Wu Tianming's *Old Well* in Tokyo (1987) and Zhang Yimou's *Red Sorghum* in Berlin (1988), but not before they had cemented the link in Politburo minds between 'new wave' films and other forms of 'dissidence'. As a result, the 'Fifth Generation' directors now face ideological pressures on top of all the economic pressures that beset them.

The situation of the 'Fifth Generation' directors in Xi'an is, of course, closely tied in with Wu Tianming's own position as studio head. Wu remains committed to financing *yishu pian* and *tansuo pian* without regard for their commercial value in the Chinese market, and the studio now has cupboards full of domestic and international prizes to testify to the high level of its artistic achievements. No one doubts that Xi'an Film Studio has become the spiritual home of the 'New Chinese Cinema'. But the studio's financial problems remain intractable, and the continuing production of innovative and non-commercial films seems less and less justifiable in strictly economic terms. Other studio heads have meanwhile abandoned production of 'New Cinema' films entirely, leaving the younger directors on their staffs with no option but to bide their time making would-be commercial entertainments. In this convoluted Catch-22, some have begun voting with their feet. As I write, the director/

scriptwriter of *King of the Children* is resident in New York and planning to shoot a film in the USA, the co-writer of the screenplay is teaching at the University of Oslo, and the author of the original short-story is living in a trailer outside Los Angeles. They are three among many who have chosen to spend time away from China.

The seven directors who have so far done most to shape and define the 'New Chinese Cinema' are Chen Kaige, Huang Jianxin, Hu Mei, Tian Zhuangzhuang, Wu Ziniu, Zhang Yimou and Zhang Zeming. Five of them were members of the Academy's Class of '82; four of them have worked with Wu Tianming in Xi'an. When the time comes to write a history of the Chinese 'new wave', it will need to chronicle their achievements, frustrations and failures. They are far from being the only film-makers in China who are fighting for a cinema of integrity and substance; their spiritual allies in the older generations include Wu Tianming, Yan Xueshu and Zhang Zi'en in Xi'an, Huang Jianzhong and Ling Zifeng in Beijing, Yang Yanjin in Shanghai and Hu Bingliu in Guangzhou – and even that list is far from exhaustive. They also have contemporaries, most of them still on the first rung of the ladder, whose work has a clear family relationship with the 'Fifth Generation' films; that list would have to include Zhou Xiaowen and Guo Fangfang in Xi'an, Peng Xiaolian and Zhang Jianya in Shanghai and Sun Zhou in Guangzhou. None the less, the seven directors picked out above constitute a viable cross-section of the 'new wave'. Their films have rewritten the grammar of Chinese cinema, and have extended its vocabulary.

CHEN KAIGE was born in Beijing, 12 August 1952. His first three years as a *zhiqing* were spent clearing forests on a rubber plantation in Yunnan Province (South-West China), where one of his workmates was Ah Cheng, future author of *King of the Children*. Chen managed to extricate himself from the plantation by joining the army, but he remained stuck in Yunnan: he was assigned to the units patrolling the border with Vietnam, already tense some eight years before the clashes that left the Chinese army bloodied and demoralized. He resigned in 1975 and managed to return to Beijing, where he found a job in the main film processing laboratory, opposite the film studio. After

his four years in the Film Academy he was assigned to the staff of Beijing Film Studio and assisted Huang Jianzhong on two major features: *The Fragile Skiff* (*Yiye Xiaozhou*, 1982) and *26 Girls* (*Ershiliu ge Guniang*, 1983). (It is perhaps not coincidental that Huang has pushed his own career in a markedly more 'experimental' direction since having Chen as a member of his team. Huang's recent films *Questions for the Living* (*Yi ge Sizhe dui Shengzhe de Fangwen*, 1986) and *Two Virtuous Women* (*Zhen Nü*, 1987) are avant-garde in form and theme.) In 1984, Chen joined his classmates Zhang Yimou and He Qun in Guangxi Film Studio, where they produced the features *Yellow Earth* and *The Big Parade* and – to make some money for themselves – the TV film *Forced Take-off* (*Qiangxing Qifei*, 1985). During the protracted argument with the authorities over the final cut of *The Big Parade*, Chen signed the agreement with Wu Tianming to make *King of the Children* for the Xi'an studio.

All three of Chen's features to date have been rooted in the experiences of his own formative years. *Yellow Earth* (*Huang Tudi*, 1984) describes the arrival of an educated man in a poor and backward peasant community – a situation with obvious resonances for all *zhiqing*. *The Big Parade* (*Da Yuebing*, 1986) examines the psychology of teenagers and others in the Chinese army, with oblique references back to the disastrous border war with Vietnam. And *King of the Children* deals directly with the experience of a *zhiqing* in Yunnan Province. *King of the Children* is discussed at length at the end of this essay; what is striking in

27

retrospect is the way that Chen's first two features clear the aesthetic ground for the innovations of the third. *Yellow Earth* and *The Big Parade*, taken together, form a kind of diptych, with one film exactly balancing and countering the other. One could draw up a binary grid of contrasts between the two films: historical versus contemporary subject, feminist concerns versus masculine values, Academy-ratio screen versus CinemaScope screen, low light levels versus bleached-out images, and so on. These patterns of contrast could be explained as evidence of film-school graduates deliberately testing the range of their own skills by making their second film as unlike their first as possible. Equally, *The Big Parade* could be seen as a pragmatic response to the commercial failure (in China) of *Yellow Earth*. At a deeper level, though, the two films are bonded by their concern with the state of the Chinese nation, their use of a microcosmic situation as a metaphor for the macrocosm, and their complementary aesthetic researches – on imagery and composition in *Yellow Earth* and on sound in *The Big Parade*.

When Chen Kaige disavows any 'political' intentions behind *Yellow Earth* (as he has done in countless interviews), he is merely stressing the distance that separates his work from the didactic, propaganda cinema of earlier years. *Yellow Earth* is, in fact, profoundly 'political' in its own, questioning way. The film's narrative deconstructs one of the Communist Party's most cherished myths, which holds that Communist ideology spread like wildfire through China's peasant communities in the 1930s – as celebrated in countless propaganda movies of the 1950s and 1960s. *Yellow Earth* centres on the 8th Route Army soldier Gu Qing, who travels from the Communist base in Yan'an to the villages of Northern Shaanxi in search of folk songs that might be adapted for use as campaign songs in the anti-Japanese war. His mission is transparently a summary and cipher of the Communist drive to win hearts and minds in the rural hinterlands. But the only direct results of Gu's ideological fieldwork are that the young child-bride Cuiqiao runs away from her elderly husband and apparently commits suicide, and that her slightly retarded younger brother Hanhan is plunged into unchannelled confusion. Gu himself is clearly taken aback by the degree of poverty and strength of feudal superstition he finds in the village, and his retreat back to Yan'an two-thirds of

28

the way through the film can only be taken as an admission of (at least temporary) defeat. The film's provocative open ending juxtaposes the peasants' prayers for rain with a ghostly echo of Cuiqiao's voice singing the song (learned from Gu Qing) that promises Communist salvation: 3,500 years of peasant tradition versus an idealistic and overdue campaign for change. By failing to resolve the contradiction, the film contrives to suggest that the issue *remains* unresolved in China, even today. Clearly, this is not an apolitical film.

The film-makers' work on imagery and composition is central to the overall meaning and effect. As cinematographer, Zhang Yimou (himself a native of Shaanxi Province, hence totally familiar with the terrain around the Yellow River and the loess plateau) chose to keep horizon lines unusually high or low in the frame, echoing a local peasant-painting tradition. The resulting 'unbalanced' compositions give the images a strong metaphorical weight: the sky becomes the 'heaven' of peasant superstition, the yellow earth itself is seen as both the origin and nemesis of

Chinese life. Wide shots are scattered liberally throughout the film, constantly underlining the links between the people, the elements and the land. More surprisingly, the principle of allowing the images to carry the bulk of the meaning is extended to the more intimate scenes involving the main characters. Dialogue is reduced to the barest minimum, and the evolving relationships are articulated more through reaction shots of faces than through words. Hanhan's expressionless face, for example, is used more than once as a *tabula rasa*, saying everything and nothing, conjuring possibilities of love, incomprehension, resignation – or a child's capacity to grasp a hitherto undreamt concept like 'change'. The crucial thing here is the element of *ambiguity*, which not only reappears in the film's refusal to tie up the various threads of meaning but also reaches into the heart of the plotting itself: should Cuiqiao's disappearance (she vanishes while crossing the Yellow River at night, her singing voice cut off in mid-syllable – the syllable in question being 'Comm . . .') be taken as suicide, misadventure or as something purely symbolic? Ambiguity was precisely the element most strenuously outlawed by Mao's 'Yan'an line' on the arts. *Yellow Earth* insists on the truth of ambiguity; at the same time, it has the wit to locate its central ambiguities in images rather than words.

After a film that hinges on the exchange of songs and redefines the language of Chinese cinema in terms closer to song than to speech, *The Big Parade* seems at first sight positively prosaic: a film about young army volunteers training for possible places in China's 1984 National Day parade. Furthermore, it is a film which trumps earlier propaganda films about the army at their own game by creating the most plausible 'collective protagonist' seen anywhere since the early Eisenstein movies. In fact, it centres on six main characters (the immature kid, the guileless peasant, the frustrated intellectual, the self-hating stoic and so on) but carefully prevents any of them from emerging as a dominant protagonist – or as a full-blooded stereotype, for that matter. The emphasis is on the squaddies as a group, because the covert concern is with what each man has to repress or sublimate in order to win his place in the parade. Chen Kaige has said that he considers it a film not about the army but about life in China today.

The film sets up a visual dialectic between the parade ground (systematically filmed in static shots or in follow shots that keep their subject centred) and the barracks (equally systematically filmed in mobile shots, bustling with uncoordinated movement). Each setting thus becomes the other's 'off-screen', the space between them being the dangerous conceptual ground where individual ambitions and aspirations clash with social expectations and demands. More subversively, the film then goes on to establish a larger dialectic between what is seen and what is heard. A stream of questioning and hesitant voice-overs cuts against the grain of the bright, assertive images, and the visual syntax often makes it hard (at least initially) to be sure *whose* voice is being heard. Visual certainties are undermined by aural uncertainties, and the disjunction helps to push the film into its symbolic register. Had Chen been allowed to end the film as he first intended – with the *sound* of the 'big parade' itself laid over images of a deserted Tiananmen Square in the centre of Beijing – then the closing moments would have provocatively reversed the terms of the dialectic: authoritative sound would have cut against a questioning image.

It's worth stressing these formalist strategies over the nuts and bolts of the film's dramatic content for two reasons. One is that they are almost entirely without precedent in Chinese cinema; you have to look all the way back to Fei Mu's 1948 film *Spring in a Small Town* (*Xiao Cheng zhi Chun*) to find a comparable determination to rethink the fundamental grammar and film language of a Chinese movie. The other reason is that they are a basic part of the *zhiqing* generation's plan to transform Chinese cinema. The rethinking of film form is not only a reaction against decades of stage-bound, dialogue-heavy Chinese movies but also an extension of the work begun in the *zhiqing* poetry of the *samizdat* magazines. Just as *Yellow Earth* deconstructs one of the founding myths of the Chinese Communist Party, so *The Big Parade* deconstructs the rhetoric of nationalism, patriotism and self-sacrifice that has dominated Chinese life since the Communist victory. Chen Kaige's films do not baldly voice opposition to the state; instead, they rephrase all the state's assertions as questions and, in semiotic terms, displace meaning from the 'signified' to the 'signifier'. Both *Yellow Earth* and *The Big Parade* are frankly exploratory films (*tansuo pian*), easily recognizable as the work of film-makers feeling their way into their *métier*. Chen Kaige consolidates and builds on their innovations in his third feature *King of the Children*, to which I return below. First, though, it is interesting to compare Chen's work with that of his *zhiqing* contemporaries in the film industry.

HU MEI was born in Beijing in September 1956. Like Chen, she was the child of cultured, intellectual parents; her father was full-time conductor for an army symphony orchestra. Inevitably, the family was decimated by the Cultural Revolution. Hu Mei was nine years old when her father was hauled away and imprisoned by Red Guards, and her upbringing was entrusted to an aunt in the city suburbs. She had no choice but to spend her teenage years striving to be a model Young Communist, and in 1975 joined an army theatre troupe as an actress. Equally, she had no choice but to repress whatever she felt about her father and his supposed crimes – until she was able to broach her feelings obliquely in her second feature, *Far From War*. Her four years at the Film Academy

(1978–82) provided her first respite from years of army 'guidance' and allowed her a space to think for herself; she reportedly coped at the time by becoming 'one of the boys' and out-swearing her male classmates, but a distinctly female sensibility surfaced as soon as she began directing. Her success has been remarkable, especially considering that she was assigned, on graduation from the Film Academy, to work in the army's own August First Film Studio in Beijing – notoriously the most 'conservative' and stifling studio in the country.

Her first feature *Army Nurse* (*Nüer Lou*, 1985) was nominally co-directed with her male classmate Li Xiaojun, who was posted to the studio alongside her. It chronicles several years in the life of Qiao Xiaoyu, a young nurse in a military hospital, centring on her 'forbidden' passion for a patient named Ding Zhu and her eventual arranged marriage to a man proposed by her leaders. The film plays like a Chinese version of *Effi Briest*: the story of a woman whose instincts are to rebel against the prevailing patriarchal order but who accepts that order at such a deep, subconscious level that she finally surrenders all sense of

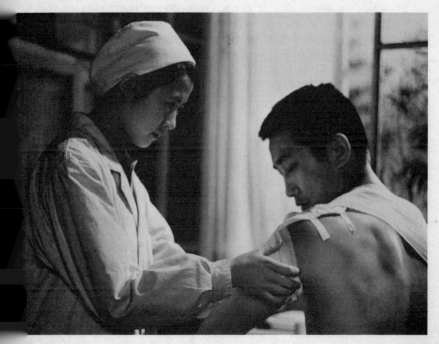

her own, independent identity. Mr Li's involvement notwithstanding, *Army Nurse* is very clearly a film made by a young woman and addressed to Chinese women of her own age. But making it for the August First Studio entailed discussing and justifying it shot-by-shot with the studio leaders, all of them men past what the West would consider to be retirement age, none of them remotely in tune with the feminist inklings of the *zhiqing* generation. It seems to have been the arduous process of negotiating the film through the studio's system of censorship and editorial supervision that turned Hu Mei's thoughts to an issue of wide-ranging relevance to China in this period of 'reform': the continuing role, if any, of first-generation Communist veterans, especially those 'old soldiers' – like her own father – who had been in Yan'an during the anti-Japanese war.

Far From War (*Yuanli Zhanzheng de Niandai*, 1987) is the product of her reflections, a film about a Yan'an veteran living with his son, daughter-in-law and grandson in present-day Beijing. The son teaches strategy in the Military Academy, which means that the family enjoys relatively comfortable housing by Beijing standards. But the apartment is too small for three generations, and the old man (a rare film appearance by the distinguished stage actor Huang Zongluo) constantly finds himself in the way of his daughter-in-law's plans for redecoration, cleaning and cooking. Hu Mei sketches the domestic situation economically, in the process depicting a 'typical' middle-class marriage with surprising candour and a great deal more plausibility than is usual in Chinese movies. But she then steers the film off in the direction of fantasy and desire. A magazine article triggers off the old man's memories of what seems to have been the one moment of real passion in his life: an erotic encounter with a peasant girl during his days as a young soldier in the anti-Japanese war. The memories are elaborated as a series of fragmented flashbacks, in much the same vein as those in a Sergio Leone movie, gradually revealing the association of sex with death in the old man's mind. As the memories overtake him, the old man sets off (without telling his family) on a forlorn and meaningless journey to the village where he met the girl. Meaningless, because the trip does nothing to exorcize the primal scene from his fantasies.

Both of these films suffered censorship at the hands of the army; neither is now viewable in quite the form that Hu Mei intended. But the relative simplicity of Hu's film language – both films are conventionally lyrical – helps them to survive this interference. No amount of cutting or tinkering can disguise the fact that both films centre on emotional blockages, a syndrome that has preoccupied more and more of China's writers but one that film-makers have tended to avoid. Hu's films take it as given that the army is synonymous with Maoist values, and explore the precise moments when individuals must choose between surrender to those values (and, by extension, 'the good of the nation') and surrender to their emotional impulses (whether familial or sexual). It is not hard to relate this syndrome to the typical *zhiqing* trauma of being forced to turn against parents and friends on ideological grounds, or to the equally typical *zhiqing* struggle between self-sacrifice and self-sufficiency. In this light, the army background to both films takes on a very particular force: it's useful to recall that all Chinese of the *zhiqing* generation were taught in their early teens to 'emulate Lei Feng' – Lei Feng being a fictitious 'model soldier' who devoted a tragically short but profoundly happy life to serving his comrades, and who gratefully accepted his role as 'a cog in the machine'. Hu Mei's films coincide with Chen Kaige's *The Big Parade* in seeing military service as a cypher for nationality in the People's Republic. But she is more concerned with specifics than Chen is, and her gentle, sympathetic portrait of the failing patriarch in *Far From War* represents the most constructive engagement yet from any member of the *zhiqing* generation with the problems of their parents' generation.

HUANG JIANXIN was born in Xi'an in 1954. Unlike other 'new wave' directors, he came through the Cultural Revolution comparatively unscathed, which is doubtless why he feels no need to re-open old wounds in his work. In his late teens he joined the army and managed to pursue a hobby of amateur photography. When China began to return to normal in the mid-1970s, he entered Xibei University to read Chinese literature. On graduation he was offered a job as script editor at Xi'an Film Studio; he became more actively involved in production after being asked to help with continuity on Ai

Shui's *The Tenth Bullet Scar* (*Dishige Dankong*, 1981), and got to
know Wu Tianming during the filming of *The River Without
Buoys* in 1983. He was nominated by the studio for a place on
one of the Film Academy's two-year intensive courses (designed
for people already working in the film industry), and spent the
years 1983–5 in Beijing. Interestingly, most of the exercises he
filmed at the Academy centred on the feelings and perceptions
of women. His final project at the Academy was a 35 mm short
feature called *Reminiscences in a Light Rain* (*Xiao Yu zhong de
Huiyi*, 1985, co-directed with Zhang Xin), about a shy girl
student's unvoiced crush on a popular boy student; the Film
Bureau banned it from domestic distribution because of its
allegedly 'negative' view of student life. On his return to Xi'an
he was immediately assigned to direct by Wu Tianming, by
then well established as the studio's head.

Huang's first two features form a diptych; indeed, they
resemble each other more than he perhaps intended. Both
sprang from a wish not to pick over the past by asking new
questions but to make films literally without precedent in
Chinese cinema. The first was *The Black Cannon Incident*

(*Heipao Shijian*, 1985), based on, but hugely different from, a
short-story by the novelist Zhang Xianliang, vice chairman of
the Chinese Writers' Association. A script already existed when
Huang was assigned to the project; with Zhang's permission, he
rewrote it and came up with something that was 50 per cent
original. The result was a tragicomic satire, relentlessly detailing
the various obstacles to reform and prosperity in present-day
China: intellectual cowardice and passivity, bureaucratic
stupidity and ideological intransigence. The film ingeniously
constructs a futuristic picture of China as a high-tech society,
only to undercut it with a storyline that shows a paranoid
misunderstanding leading to a costly industrial disaster. The
protagonist is a humble, chess-playing mining engineer named
Zhao Shuxin, a middle-aged bachelor with a number of question
marks in his file, including his devoutly Catholic parentage and
his ability to speak German. The problems arise from a telegram
innocently sent by Zhao to ask a friend to return a missing
chess-piece, and rapidly escalate into a battle of wills between a
pragmatic works manager and a fervently Marxist–Leninist
Deputy Party Secretary, the latter a woman with an abiding
distrust of all things foreign and a 'type' all too recognizable in
Chinese political life. The chapter of errors that follows hinges
on a delicious irony: Zhao, it is decided, must be prevented
from working with a visiting German expert *for his own
protection*, since current Party policy is to trust and respect
intellectuals. And so the German loses his specialist translator,
and the company squanders its investment in imported
machinery.

Zhao Shuxin, the likeable klutz who abjectly submits to
decisions from above, proved so popular with the Chinese
audience that Huang Jianxin decided to bring the character
back in a follow-up. *The Stand-In* (*Cuowei*, 1986, also known in
English as *Dislocation*) finds Zhao installed as managing director
of a giant corporation, so inundated with bureaucratic
commitments that he dreams of inventing a robot double of
himself to take his place at meetings and conferences. *Black
Cannon* gained a lot of its point from being set in 1983 and
showing it as if it were 2003, a futuristic present in which social
and economic problems have been overcome but political
problems remain. *The Stand-In* abandons all reference to

Chinese realities and plays as all-out science-fiction comedy –
with a marked loss in satirical edge. Despite a heroic
performance in the lead by Liu Zifeng (an actor discovered by
Huang Jianxin in the Shanghai Children's Art Theatre, after a
long search for his ideal 'Zhao Shuxin'), the film contents itself
with its vein of 'absurdism' and never faces up to the
implications of the character's incipient schizophrenia.

The elements of satire in *Black Cannon* and *The Stand-In*
were not entirely new in Chinese cinema, although it's necessary
to look back to a banned comedy of 1957 to find anything as
scathing in its line of attack. What *is* new in both films is a *mise
en scène* founded on stylized design and a carefully restricted
colour palette. Huang and his art director and cinematographer
set out to eliminate green and blue from their spectrum, leaving
a world of blacks and whites shot through with warning reds
and sickly yellows. Their schema works magnificently in *Black
Cannon*, where it produces all kinds of metaphorical overtones
in a fundamentally naturalistic diegesis, but becomes merely
schematic in *The Stand-In*, where neither the budget nor the
film-makers' imaginations is up to the challenge of inventing an
imagined future. Their innovative approach to visual meaning

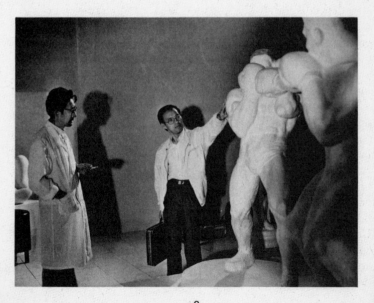

added the word *huangdan* (the absurd) to the Chinese critical
vocabulary, and paved the way for films like Huang Jianzhong's
Questions for the Living and Wang Jixing's extraordinary
children's movie *Visions from a Jail Cell* (*Moku zhong de
Huanxiang*, 1987). Of all the Chinese 'new wave' films, these
'absurdist' movies have least to do with the Cultural Revolution
and its traumas, but their spirit of aggressive innovation, their
determination to 'do different' seems entirely characteristic of
the exasperation with traditional culture felt by many of the
younger intellectuals who lived through the 'ten chaotic years'.
Huang Jianxin, though, consistently looks forward rather than
back. Not surprisingly, his third feature *Samsara* (in progress at
the time of writing) is a collaboration with Wang Shuo, a
talented young writer so far ignored by the Beijing literary
establishment.

TIAN ZHUANGZHUANG was born in Beijing in 1952. Both his
father Tian Fang and his mother Yu Lan were well-known film
actors in the years before the Cultural Revolution; Yu Lan is
now head of the Children's Film Studio in Beijing. His early life
quite closely paralleled Chen Kaige's: his *zhiqing* years (from
1968) were spent in Jilin Province, once part of Manchuria, and
he extricated himself from the fields by joining the army. He
managed to return to city life by securing an apprenticeship in
the photographic department of the Agricultural Film Unit,
where he worked on a number of instructional films and
documentaries. He won his place at the Film Academy in 1978,
and distinguished himself while there by co-directing the video-
film *Our Corner* (*Women de Jiaoluo*, 1980, made in collaboration
with fellow students Xie Xiaojing and Cui Xiaoqin); the tape
was based on a short-story by the young writer Jin Shui, who
had fallen victim to a paralysing illness during his own years as
a *zhiqing*, and it was hailed at the time as a sign of the potential
links between the new literature and the hoped-for new cinema.
On graduation, Tian was assigned to Beijing Film Studio, which
had no work for him but sensibly left him free to look for
projects elsewhere. His first feature as co-director was the
children's film *Red Elephant*, noted earlier in this essay. After
that, he made the TV film *A Summer Experience* (*Xiatian de
Jingli*, 1983) and then became a nomad, roaming from one

39

regional studio to the next, making films as he went. To gain experience, he accepted an offer from the tiny Kunming Film Studio to direct *September* (*Jiuyue*, 1984), a shamelessly sentimental melodrama about a children's choir, a music teacher on the eve of retirement and a reformed convict.

His international reputation – at home, his notoriety – rests on his next two features. The first was *On the Hunting Ground* (*Liechang Zhasa*, 1985), made for the Inner Mongolia Film Studio; the second was *Horse Thief* (*Daoma Zei*, 1986), made for Wu Tianming in Xi'an. Both are deliberately gnomic portraits of minority nationalities in China, seen without the usual mediating presence of Han Chinese characters. *On the Hunting Ground* is almost entirely plotless, and conspicuously fails to explain the workings of the *zhasa* hunting code that governs the Mongolian plains – a code at least as obscure to Chinese viewers as to western viewers. (Indeed, putting the term in the film's Chinese title was already provocative, since few outside Mongolia have ever heard of it.) In so far as the film has a narrative centre, it deals with a hunter's transgression of the code and his subsequent penance. But it is obvious that Tian's prime concern is with the rituals, patterns and rhythms of the tribe, and much of his film could easily pass for documentary.

Horse Thief takes a similar (and similarly minimal) plot and locates it in Tibet; the transgressor this time is a rustler and highway bandit who is expelled from his tribe for his crimes but who recognizes no higher authority but the Buddhist church. The film spans the year from the death of the horse thief's son as he and his wife begin life as nomads to the birth of their second son and the man's decision to sacrifice himself for the sake of his family. Their wanderings bring them to many of the major Tibetan Buddhist festivals (including the Xodoin Festival, where they are transfixed by the sight of the traditional dance dramas with their child actors in skull masks), allowing Tian to exercise his penchant for documentary filming and recording ceremonies that were all but wiped out in the Cultural Revolution. The entire film resolves itself into a meditation on life and death in the Buddhist scheme of things: it opens with images of a 'sky burial', the dismemberment and laying out of human remains so that vultures may carry them up into the heavens, and closes with an image of blood on the snow, the

only trace of the robbery in which the horse thief deliberately sought his own death. It should be noted that *Horse Thief* has not been released in quite the form that Tian intended. The Film Bureau insisted on trimming both 'sky burial' sequences, fearing that Tibetan sensibilities might be offended by Tian's frankness about the physical details of the rite, and also insisted on adding the opening caption that sets the film in '1923'. Tian himself had intended the period to be non-specific, hence timeless.

Both of these remarkable movies have complex roots in the director's *zhiqing* years. Most obviously, their naked curiosity about the ways and lives of minority races springs from the experience of being sent into a backward, rural community, far from Beijing. Equally, though, they stand as implicit critiques of the 'national minority film' genre that flowered – the word is chosen advisedly – in the cinema of the 1950s, where its transparently phoney vein of folksy romance offered a measure of respite from the drabness of most propaganda cinema. The almost ethnographic character of Tian's films is clearly related to his impatience with the genre's usual utopian fabrications, and thus constitutes another facet of the 'Fifth Generation' reaction against earlier norms of Chinese cinema. But the most fundamental challenge posed by the films is their emphasis on the capacity of Chinese people, of whatever race or ethnic background, to submit to systems of control – systems that may be as irrational and obscure as the human behaviour they sometimes provoke. It takes little imagination to see that this is a topic of obsessive interest to the *zhiqing* generation, who moved from blind faith in Maoism to a kind of pragmatic pessimism via an enforced crash course in *realpolitik*. Tian has said: 'Both films may seem to deal with national minorities, but in reality they refer to the fate of the Chinese nation as a whole.'

Neither *On the Hunting Ground* nor *Horse Thief* has been given any noticeable distribution in China, and Tian got himself into trouble by telling a Chinese interviewer that he didn't care whether or not audiences saw his work now because he was making it for the twenty-first century. (Werner Herzog once said something similar in the West, where he got away with it unchallenged.) Tian's wounded aggression, of course, arises from the profound frustrations he faces in trying to make films that resist the expectations of audiences, distributors and exhibitors alike. In the event, the outcry that his remarks provoked in the film industry had the effect of forcing him to back down and tackle more orthodox commercial projects. His nominal home studio in Beijing suddenly found work for him, directing a straightforward literary drama based on Lao She's novel *The Drum Singers* (*Gushu Yiren*, 1987). The film, which deals with the sufferings of artists during the years of the anti-Japanese war, is known in English as *The Street Players*. More recently, he has been working on a movie about Chinese teenagers' fascination with breakdancing. In short, he now finds himself in much the same position as many independent film-makers in western countries: biding his time and trying to earn a crust while looking for the opportunity to return to subjects that he cares about.

WU ZINIU was born in Leshan, Sichuan Province, in November 1953. An early interest in painting and poetry was just beginning to coalesce into a passion for cinema when the Cultural Revolution relegated him to the fields. By 1978, when he sat the entrance exam for the Film Academy, he had found his way back to Leshan and was working with a small theatre group. His four years at the Academy gave him a solid grounding in Soviet film theory and exposed him to movies as diverse as Antonioni's *Blow-Up* and Resnais's *Hiroshima, Mon Amour*. On graduation he was lucky enough to be assigned to the small Xiaoxiang Film Studio in Changsha, the capital of Hunan Province. He turned down a request to work as assistant to an established but none too talented woman director, and was instead allowed to begin directing episodes for a TV series called *Beautiful Youth* (*Piaoliang de Qingnian*). In June 1983 he began work on his first feature, *The Candidate*, dealt with earlier in this essay. He has worked as prolifically as possible ever since, but his career has been blighted by censorship wrangles of various sorts. His association with the Xiaoxiang Studio ended (amicably) after his fourth feature, and he now works as a semi-freelance director, taking interesting work wherever he can find it. He is currently completing a two-part film about the turbulent lives of southern farmers in the 1930s, based on novels by Sima Wensen and financed by the small but ambitious Fujian Film Studio.

Like other *zhiqing* born and raised in country towns, Wu Ziniu was less scarred by the Cultural Revolution than his big-city contemporaries were, and his films are correspondingly less marked by direct traces of his years in the countryside than many. What seems none the less highly characteristic of his age and background is the strain of sheer contrariness in his work: his capacity for going against convention and 'received wisdom', and for stubbornly clinging to his point of view, no matter what opposition it runs into. This was already apparent in his second feature *Secret Decree* (*Diexue Heigu*, literally 'Bloodshed in the Dark Valley', 1984), which broke distinctly new ground by taking a KMT officer as its hero – albeit a KMT officer who resists Chiang Kai-shek's capitulation to the invading Japanese army in the 1930s. This modest provocation aside, the film concretely established war as the 'natural' milieu for a Wu Ziniu film; like

Sam Fuller, he maintains an unimpeachable anti-war stance, while seeing 'drama' as being synonymous with 'conflict' in a way that makes his choice of war subjects and metaphors inevitable.

It was doubtless this proclivity that led him into his ill-fated third feature *The Dove Tree* (*Gezi Shu*, 1985), a film set on the Yunnan–Vietnam border and concerning the 1979 clashes and punitive strikes of the Chinese and Vietnamese armies. Since its humiliation in those clashes, the Chinese PLA has been sensitive to the point of acute paranoia to all references to them in the Chinese media, both factual and fictional, and by the time that Wu's film was approaching completion the army had managed to attack and suppress the short-story on which the film was based. The finished film was consequently rushed straight from the Xiaoxiang Studio to Beijing, where it reputedly bypassed the usual Film Bureau vetting and went direct to the highest level of government for inspection. There are countless rumours and anecdotes about what happened at that screening; the best has Deng Xiaoping himself breaking the stony silence after the film by remarking that it had obvious commercial potential in Vietnam. Whatever was actually said, the fact is that the film vanished overnight. Around the same time, the PLA was also gunning for Chen Kaige's *The Big Parade*, partly because it, too, contained references to China's moral defeat in the border war. In recent years, in fact, the army has been increasingly concerned to 'protect' its public image, and it has never hesitated to go above the heads of the Film Bureau to suppress scripts and movies of which it disapproves. Typically, Wu Ziniu rose to this bait by opting to make his fifth feature for the army's own film studio in Beijing. Wu saw *Evening Bell* (*Wan Zhong*, 1988) as a reprise of the themes of *The Dove Tree*, but set more safely back in the years of the anti-Japanese war. His strategy was not subtle enough to save the film from an eighteen-month wrangle over the exact form of the final cut; the film had to pass through four stages of censorship, three of them within the army, and it underwent modification at every single stage.

In 1986, Wu had rushed his fourth feature *The Last Day of Winter* (*Zuihou yi ge Dongri*) into production, partly to help himself get over the trauma of the banning of *The Dove Tree* and partly to help the Xiaoxiang Studio recoup the losses it

sustained by producing a film denied distribution. At first sight, *Last Day* looks like a quintessential *zhiqing* film: the opening scene shows a train arriving in a station in the back of beyond and disgorging three obviously urban types – a man, a woman and a little girl – who soon join up to negotiate the inhospitable terrain together. However, as soon as it becomes apparent that the three strangers have all come to visit relatives in China's *gulag* – a vast labour camp in the wilds of Xinjiang – the film leaves behind its echoes of the *zhiqing* experience and opts for a weird blend of stylized realism (the framing story) and stylized melodrama (the flashbacks to the crimes that led the prisoners into custody). The focus on sibling relationships is unusual in Chinese cinema, and the film contains several passages of bravura brilliance, but Wu never fully succeeds in subverting the age-old conventions of the prison movie. Still, the film is rich in details that could have come from the imagination of a 'Fifth Generation' director. When, for instance, the male visitor finds his delinquent sister tending a herd of sheep on the sparse grasslands outside the prison building, Wu films their sad, wordless encounter in a long-held wide-angle shot that eventually shows the woman breaking down as her brother unpacks the gift he has brought her: a supply of sanitary towels to last her for the months and years to come . . .

Wu Ziniu's combative and iconoclastic vision sets him apart from most of his contemporaries, as does his full-blooded interest in storytelling *per se*. Of all the *zhiqing* film-makers, he seems the one most ready to transmute first-person experience into third-person fiction. This makes for robust, materialist film-making, strongly anchored in physical realities and founded on a matter-of-fact perception of everything from moral fallibility to bodily functions. Chen Kaige is perhaps the only other director who manages to combine this kind of candour with a formalist sensibility that inflects his sense of composition and framing. But Wu is clearly more flexible than Chen, and his readiness to make the best of available options while still maintaining his contrary point-of-view may yet prove to equip him better for survival in the Chinese film industry, whatever directions it takes in the years to come.

ZHANG YIMOU was born in Xi'an in 1950. He had just completed his time in Middle School when the Cultural Revolution began; he spent three years in the countryside and then seven working in a factory. Early enthusiasms for drawing, taking photographs and watching movies led him to apply for a place in the cinematography department of the Film Academy in 1978; as noted earlier, he was initially refused on grounds of age but then admitted after his direct appeal to the Ministry of Culture. By his own account, he began sensing the likelihood that he would eventually turn director about halfway through his four years in the Academy. On graduation he was assigned to the Guangxi Film Studio, where his first three features as cinematographer were *The One and the Eight*, *Yellow Earth* and *The Big Parade*. He effected the transition from cinematography to directing by means of a move from Guangxi to Xi'an Film Studio. Wu Tianming invited him to come (home) to Xi'an to photograph *Old Well*; Zhang agreed, on condition that Wu would let him go on to direct a film himself. As things turned

47

out, Zhang ended up not only shooting but also playing the lead
role in *Old Well*. And his début film as director, *Red Sorghum*,
became the first 'Fifth Generation' movie to win mass-audience
acceptance in China.

Zhang's creative input into the films he photographed is
impossible to measure. I have already noted that his
contribution to *The One and the Eight* seems to have been
greater than that of its director Zhang Junzhao; and it is clear
that *Yellow Earth* was at least as 'personal' to him as it was to
Chen Kaige, not least because it was filmed in the landscapes
where he was born and raised. It is easier to sense what he
brought to *Old Well* through his performance as Sun
Wangquan, the first young man in his Shaanxi village to train in
a technical college and hence the first to bring a scientific eye to
the problem of digging a water-bearing well in a chronically arid
region. Zhang's performance works to mitigate the lingering
tendency towards melodrama in Wu Tianming's direction and
helps to turn what might in other hands have been unpromising
material into a searching account of some fundamental strengths
and weaknesses in the Chinese character. Both film and

performance are particularly strong in facing up to the implications of China's pervasive sexual repressiveness: Confucian/Communist taboo against adultery and sex before marriage, which produces a vein of retarded adolescence and emotional immaturity that can stunt entire lives permanently.

Red Sorghum (*Hong Gaoliang*, 1987) suggests a rather unexpected character for Zhang as a director. It is clearly a 'photographer's film', in the sense that its lush pictorial values and carefully thought-through colour scheme sometimes outweigh its dramatic content. (Zhang entrusted the cinematography to his classmate Gu Changwei, who also shot *King of the Children*.) Alongside Chen Kaige's patrician meditations on the state of the nation, though, *Red Sorghum* is a proletarian belch of a film: a blend of folk-tale and black comedy interspersed with raucous marriage and drinking songs. It derives from two short-stories by the Shandong writer Mo Yan, and chronicles the meeting and marriage of a couple who will become the unseen narrator's grandparents, and the birth of their son who will become the narrator's father. It opens with an arranged marriage and semi-forcible seduction outside the marriage, and ends in the carnage of the Japanese invasion in the 1930s. The colour red runs through the film as a leitmotiv, from the bridal sedan to the sorghum-based liquor distilled in the winery the heroine inherits to the blood shed in the anti-Japanese resistance.

The choice of a rural subject no doubt reflects Zhang's still-latent *zhiqing* sensibilities, but the film seems in other respects unrelated to the main currents of 'Fifth Generation' cinema. Its central thrust is its celebration of a man and woman who bow to no morality but dare to follow their own desires. Constructing characters like this of course involves repressing the dour realities of Chinese peasant life emphasized in films like *Yellow Earth* and *Old Well*. The film's outsize visual rhetoric is Zhang's acknowledgement that what he is making is, in its double-edged way, a wish-fulfilment fantasy. And the way that the action is related to songs that are close in sound and form to traditional Shandong opera (two of them – the sedan-carriers' song and the song to the god of wine – have lyrics by Zhang Yimou himself) gives the film an implied polemic thrust: this is not the way we were, it suggests, but the way *we should have been*.

49

The degree of self-awareness behind the film can be gauged by the changes Zhang made to the original Mo Yan stories. In Mo Yan's version, 'Grandfather' is a bandit with a gang of followers; the role defines his immoral and anti-social attitudes and explains his practised ability to hold his own in fights. By turning the character into an ordinary sedan-chair carrier, Zhang Yimou liberates his psychology at a stroke. 'Grandfather' ceases to be a stereotype and becomes instead a fantastically idiosyncratic individual, a recognizable peasant type who is not a victim of feudalism but a sexual braggart and an impetuous adventurer, as likely to lose a fight as to win it. Where the film falls down is in its closing stages: the attempt to use the invading Japanese as an abstract life-negating force runs aground on the gruesome fidelity to historical fact, thereby compromising the sense of fable so lovingly elaborated elsewhere in the film.

Zhang has recently completed his second film as director, *Meizhou Bao Xingdong* (1988; literally 'The American Panther Strikes'), which is said to be a far more orthodox commercial venture, a suspense drama about an aircraft hijack designed to help Wu Tainming out of some of his current financial difficulties at the Xi'an Studio. But, however the new film turns out, Zhang has already set the pattern for one line of development in Chinese cinema with *Red Sorghum*. Whether he has, in the process, made things harder for his more cerebral 'Fifth Generation' contemporaries remains to be seen.

ZHANG ZEMING was born in Fuzhou, Fujian Province, in 1951. He was brought up in the city of Guangzhou (formerly Canton), where his mother was a director of documentaries and his father a playwright and scriptwriter. As a consequence, a lot of his childhood was spent in and around the city's Pearl River Film Studio. The Cultural Revolution decimated the family: his father was arrested as a 'KMT agent', his mother was sent off to a 'cadre school', and he himself became an anarchic Red Guard. (He recalls stealing both a car and a gun soon after the removal of his parents.) He was 'tamed' in 1968, when the authorities sent him to work in Hainan Island, off China's South-west coast. He did not manage to return to the city until ten years later, when the authorities began recruiting workers to ease a

sudden labour shortage in Guangzhou. He drifted back to the film studio and was able to rejoin his mother when she returned (as studio librarian) in 1979. By then he had already sat (and failed) the 1978 entrance exam to the Beijing Film Academy, and so he embarked on a career as a production assistant, eventually rising to the position of continuity recorder on Wang Weiyi's *Three Family Alley* (*San Jia Xiang*, 1982). He reapplied to the Film Academy in 1983, and was again rejected. He would then have faced many more years on the ladder of production management had it not been for the establishment in 1984 of the 'Youth Production Units' at the Guangxi and Xiaoxiang studios. None of the 'Fifth Generation' Academy graduates had been assigned to the Pearl River Studio in 1982, and so the field was clear for the studio's younger staff to pressure the studio heads to set up a 'Youth Unit' of their own. The only significant beneficiary of this development was Zhang Zeming, who was able to make his first feature *Swan Song* (*Juexiang*) in 1985. He has gone on to make a two-part TV film called *Aunt Dan* (*Dan Yi*, 1986) and his second feature, *The Sun and the Rain* (*Taiyang Yu*, 1987).

Like *King of the Children*, *Swan Song* derives from a short-story by a writer whose experiences as a *zhiqing* matched the director's own. In Zhang's case, the writer was Kong Jiesheng,

another Guangzhou teenager who had been sent to labour in Hainan. The story concerns the fragmented family of an elderly Cantonese musician; the old man's son, an ex-Red Guard, is reconciled with his estranged mother and sister only after his father's death in the Cultural Revolution. Zhang was relatively unfamiliar with Cantonese music, but responded strongly to both the story's deeply Cantonese flavour and the echoes of his own experiences, particularly the loss of his father. He scripted the film himself, changing many details to bring the story even closer to his own life and eliminating the gratuitous 'happy ending' of the final reconciliation. The result was a remarkable – and remarkably pessimistic – account of two decades under Communist government, seen through the grid of

disappointments, frustrations and betrayals that mark the
father's declining years. With a visual sophistication still rare in
Chinese cinema, Zhang underlines the continuity from father to
son, but only in order to stress the chasm that separates them:
the chasm between an old idealist who never fully grasped the
changing realities of his situation and a young pragmatist who
takes some knocks himself but finally adjusts all too well to the
moral imperatives of his times.

Thanks to its sensitivity to the plight of both father and son,
and its keen sense of all that has been lost in Cantonese culture
over the years, *Swan Song* stands as the most moving reflection
on the Cultural Revolution (and its prequel and aftermath) in
Chinese cinema. If it has an obvious weakness, it is merely that
its determination to avoid being seen *simply* as a chronicle of
changing times sometimes pushes it into an unnecessarily
oblique treatment of events, and leads Zhang to fall back on
some rather studied 'literary' metaphors. These minor flaws in
Swan Song become major problems in Zhang's TV film *Aunt
Dan*, but there is no trace of them in his second feature *The Sun
and the Rain*. In a sense, the latter picks up where *Swan Song*
left off: with a picture of the lives of young people in South

China's cities, which increasingly resemble Hong Kong. The film has much the same faintly glacial elegance as movies by Zhang's Taiwanese contemporary Edward Yang – and the same unerring ability to pinpoint the images and sounds that define dreams, aspirations and attitudes to life. Zhang's protagonist this time is a young woman librarian in Shenzhen (one of the new 'Special Economic Zones'). The film measures the downswing of her failing affair with a brash and self-confident advertising agent against the upswing of her nervous infatuation with a rather vulgar teenage girl student. It catches a certain contemporary urban mood with extraordinary precision, and with a surprising amount of humour. But the studio gave Zhang only half the budget of *Swan Song* to make it, and has made it known that it wants no more 'art films' from him for the time being. His *zhiqing* days seem well and truly over.

Just as surely as *Yellow Earth* opened a chapter for the 'Fifth Generation' film-makers, so Chen Kaige's third film, *King of the Children* (*Haizi Wang*, 1987), closes it. Where all earlier *zhiqing* films – including *Sacrificed Youth* (*Qingchun Ji*, 1985) by the 'Fourth Generation' woman director Zhang Nuanxin – had used the experience of being sent to the remote countryside as a means of constructing a political and moral point-of-view, *King of the Children* narrows its focus to the specific implications of the *zhiqing* experience itself – and finds them almost infinite. Chen's film is based on a short-story by Ah Cheng (Zhong Acheng), widely considered the definitive literary statement on the trials and unexpected rewards of the *zhiqing* experience. Chen Kaige, who laboured alongside Ah Cheng for three years on the rubber plantation in Yunnan Province, has adapted and modified the story to turn it into the equally definitive film. In the process, he has consolidated his experiments with the vocabulary and grammar of Chinese cinema.

King of the Children (the title is an obsolete Chinese term for 'teacher') deals with the experiences of a typical *zhiqing*, nicknamed Lao Gar ('Beanpole' might be the nearest equivalent) by his fellow exiles from the cities. It opens at the moment when his team leader informs him that he has been arbitrarily drafted into service as a teacher at the nearest village school, pauses to examine the reactions of his workmates in the commune, and then turns its attention almost exclusively to his life in his new home and in the classroom. The dramatic nub of his experience is that he comes to reject rote learning and starts encouraging his final-year pupils to write creatively, only to be fired for his pains. These basic plot-points certainly form an important part of the film's meaning, but its cinematic nexus lies elsewhere. Chen indicates that this is to be the case in his opening shot: a time-lapse shot of the thatched school buildings, perched on a hilltop, from dawn to dusk. Both image and soundtrack conjure up a world in flux: ever-changing light, buzzing clouds, drifting smoke, distant cries, snatches of song, the dull thud of wood-chopping. At the centre of it all, though, stands the school, stable and unchanging: a temple of Chinese culture. The film proceeds to demonstrate, still through an intricate flux of images and sounds, the need to tear the temple down.

At the heart of Chen Kaige's vision (as distinct from Ah Cheng's) is the figure of the mute cowherd, the boy who never comes to school. (He does not appear in the original story.) Lao Gar first notices him outside the school while he is 'teaching' Lesson 4 from his Cultural Revolution textbook, 'To be a New Peasant in the New Era'. In the course of chalking up the text on the blackboard, Lao Gar spontaneously uses a kind of shorthand that is quite common in informal written Chinese. In this particular case, he combines the written characters for 'cattle' and 'water' to form a composite character, which he intends to signify 'cattlepiss'. While the schoolchildren are faithfully copying down the text, Lao Gar's attention wanders and he becomes conscious of the young cowherd outside. His mind drifts off on a wave of cowbells and cattle-calls. He is brought back to reality by the realization that most of his pupils cannot read most of what he had chalked on the board, and by the criticism from his brightest pupil, Wang Fu, that he is failing as a teacher because he introduces unfamiliar words without explaining them. The scene ends on a note of embarrassment, as Lao Gar erases the composite character he has invented.

Each subsequent appearance of the cowherd and his cattle – either in picture or, more often, on the soundtrack – is more hallucinatory. The boy speaks to his cattle but ignores Lao Gar's questions; it is as if he represents a state of existence that is somehow outside language. Inevitably, Lao Gar comes to associate the cowherd with his invented composite character. He ends his final class by explaining his shorthand invention to the pupils – and recommending them to 'renew' language for themselves. He also tells them an anecdote from his own experiences on the commune as a cowherd: his discovery that awkward or crazed cattle can be pacified by the cowherd's urine, since cattle love its salty taste. Then, as he leaves the school for the last time and passes through the 'forest' of burnt and suggestively shaped tree stumps, he has his final vision of the boy cowherd, pissing for his cattle. Or is it another hallucination? Meanwhile, all around, the landscape burns – just as China did at the height of the Cultural Revolution.

And so Chen has a counter-schema cutting across the film's main narrative thrust: a pattern of visual and aural

hallucinations clustered around the conflict between language and non-language. Details throughout the film contribute to this pattern, from the taciturnity of the team leader in the opening scene to Wang Fu's berserk project to copy out the dictionary and then move on to a larger dictionary and copy that out too. Or from the never-ending story chanted by the commune *zhiqing* when they visit Lao Gar in the school to the inexplicable sounds that haunt Lao Gar when he's alone at night. The conflict has no resolution; the film simply holds the dialectic in suspension. But if it's clear that the 'non-language' side of the issue yields a Pandora's box of mysteries, fears and uncertainties, then it's equally clear that the 'language' side boils down to propaganda messages, rote learning and other never-ending stories. And it couldn't be clearer where Chen Kaige's sympathies lie.

Is it necessary to stress that film-making with this degree of visual and aural complexity, this density of nuance, is rare not only in Chinese cinema but in every other national cinema too? The film's final words are Lao Gar's, and they are written. First, there is the message he leaves for Wang Fu, with the gift of the dictionary: 'Wang Fu, never copy anything again, not even the dictionary.' Then there is his invented composite character for 'cattlepiss', alone at the centre of the blackboard. Not so much 'language' versus 'non-language' as 'orthodox language' versus 'new vocabulary'. China needed new vocabulary, and so did Chinese cinema.

The quotations from film-makers in this essay are all taken from conversations with the author that took place in 1986–8. Some are taken from material recorded for (but not necessarily used in) my TV documentary 'New Chinese Cinema' (1988). For all kinds of help in preparing the essay, I'd like to thank Shan Dongbing, Zhang Tielin, Wang Dingyi, Zhang Dan and Paul Clark . . . and, of course, the film-makers themselves.

T.R.

King of the Children

CHEN KAIGE AND WAN ZHI

based on the short-story 'Haizi Wang' by Ah Cheng

Edited and translated by Bonnie S. McDougall

TRANSLATOR'S NOTE

The following translation is based on the *taiben* (shooting script) corresponding to the first complete version of the film as passed for release by the authorities in August 1987. The translation has been revised according to the version of the film released in Great Britain in autumn 1988. I have also abbreviated the camera instructions and added more description of places and things unfamiliar in the West.

In August 1987, by agreement with the director, I prepared a set of subtitles for the film. These subtitles were later replaced by another set provided by the Chinese Film Import and Export Corporation. My translation of the song sung by the children at the end of the film, however, has been adopted by the Corporation without acknowledgement.

I wish to thank Ren Xiaoping, who prepared a draft translation of the original short-story for me and who also helped on the film script. I also thank Chen Kaige and Chen Maiping (Wan Zhi) for their assistance with the translation. Anders Hansson gave invaluable assistance with an inchoate manuscript. I am also very grateful to Betty Chandler in Peking and Betty Burch in Cambridge, Mass., without whose kind hospitality the translation could not have been completed.

I am also most grateful to Tony Rayns, who made available to me a copy of the British release version of the film, and to Walter Donohue of Faber and Faber for all his help and encouragement.

B.MCD.
September 1988

The film *King of the Children* is adapted from a novel of the
same name by Ah Cheng. The story is set in rural China during
the Great Cultural Revolution. The heroes of the story are a
young man who came from the city and a group of village
schoolchildren.

In 1968, two years after the Cultural Revolution had begun,
Mao issued a call to urban Chinese youths, asking them to go to
the countryside. He wanted them to live with peasants and be
re-educated by them; he wanted them to change rural China.
This call soon became a compulsive requirement; tens of
millions of urban youths between the ages of fifteen and twenty
went to rural China, leaving their parents and the city, giving
up their student life to begin life on the farms.

This movement amounted to nothing less than a major
migration of urban Chinese population; it changed the lives of
an entire generation of people and lasted for more than ten
years. These young people, who were born when the People's
Republic was founded, suffered unimaginable hardship, which
left permanent scars in their memories. However, these urban
youths also finally had a chance to witness the reality of life in
China. Their experience has an important bearing on the
changes that are occurring now in the country.

Like the urban youths depicted in *King of the Children*, Ah
Cheng and I went to live in rural China at that time.

Many would say the Cultural Revolution has destroyed
Chinese culture since numerous cultural relics were destroyed.
However, intellectually, it was more a time when the values
inherent in traditional Chinese culture were carried to a
dangerous extreme. This was violently reflected in the behaviour
of every individual – from their blind worship of the leader/
emperor figure to the total desecration and condemnation of
individual rights. These are mere repetitions of tradition.

Repetition is a characteristic of Chinese traditional culture. The children in the film copied the textbook, then the dictionary, without any comprehension. Man, in his preservation of himself, has developed culture, but in the end, the culture has become the master of man. The glory of past cultural accomplishments have left today's men impotent. With 5000 years of culture shining in our history, we had the frenzy of the 'Great Cultural Revolution'.

Thus, what is embedded in the film *King of the Children* is my judgement on traditional culture. The burning of the wasted mountains at the end of the film is a metaphor of my attitude towards traditional values. 'Don't copy anything, not even the dictionary'; 'Carry your head high on your shoulders and write your own essays' is what I require and expect of myself.

I did not directly depict the violent social confrontations that took place during the Cultural Revolution. Instead, I chose to use the language of film to create the atmosphere of the era. The forest, the fog and the sound of trees being chopped down are all reflections of China during that period of time. I thought, perhaps, that is enough.

CHEN KAIGE

King of the Children was first screened at the ICA cinema in
September 1988. The cast included:

LAO GAR, 'King of the Children'	Xie Yuan
WANG FU	Yang Xuewen
HEADMASTER CHEN	Chen Shaohua
LAIDI	Zhang Caimei
LAO HEI	Xu Guoqing
COWHERD	Le Gang
PRODUCTION TEAM LEADER	Tan Tuo
COMRADE WU	Gu Changwei
CLASS MONITOR	Wu Xia
WANG QITONG, Wang Fu's father	Liu Haichen
LAO GAR'S FRIENDS	Quiang Xiaolu, Wu Di, Sun Jianjun, He Jianzhong, Jia Tianji, Gao Bo
SCHOOLCHILDREN	The children of Mengxing State Farm Middle School, Mengla, Yunnan

Director of Photography	Gu Changwei
Production Designer	Chen Shaohua
Editor/Sound Editor	Liu Miaomiao
Music	Qu Xiaosong
Sound Recording	Tao Jing, Gu Changning
Script	Chen Kaige, Wan Zhi
Executive Producer	Wu Tainming
Director	Chen Kaige

Produced by the Xi'an Film Studio, Xi'an, China

A dense mass of Chinese characters of different styles and periods, over which is written in white: XI'AN FILM STUDIO

EXT. LOOKING DOWN AT THE SCHOOL FROM A MOUNTAIN
SIDE. FROM DAWN TO DUSK
Time-lapse shot.
Daybreak. Mist. The sound of cowbells, and the distant cry of a cowherd. Mountains gradually appear through the mist. Mist swirls between the mountains, cloaking the thatched huts which make up the school buildings. From offscreen comes the sound of wild singing. The ground gets brighter and the thatched huts gradually appear through gaps in the clouds and mist. It becomes clear enough to see a hilltop enclosed by mountains, on top of which the thatched huts are scattered like recumbent cattle. Outside the huts is a clearing which exposes the red earth. A path winds downhill like a vein through the green grass. As clouds drift to and fro, the brown school huts darken and lighten in turn. As the sun shines straight down the school seems enveloped in a heat haze. The setting sun is held between the mountain peaks. The mountains and the school are dyed orange. The western sky is a mass of rose-red clouds. Gradually the school darkens. The setting sun disappears and the mountains darken. In the twilight the mountains are dark shapes with a crimson tinge on the peaks. Offscreen the wild singing dies away.

CREDITS
The title appears in crimson letters on a tattered page from an old-fashioned Chinese book with vertical printing: KING OF THE
CHILDREN. *The title remains on screen as the credits change. Sound of chalk on blackboard, out of shot. The credits fade, the title fades, and only the tattered page remains.*

INT. THE TEAM LEADER'S HOME. DAY
This scene is one continuous fixed-angle shot.
The interior of a thatched hut, with walls made of split bamboo. It
is dark inside the hut, and shafts of sunlight through the cracks in the
walls pick out the crude furnishings. The TEAM LEADER *is sitting to*
the left on a low bamboo stool. His face is dark and his head is
closely shaven. With his bare feet resting on the ground, he is
smoking a long bamboo water pipe. Towards the back is an old tree
stump, on top of which is a sheet of paper held down by a clod of
earth. To the right there is a neat square of light formed by sunlight
coming in through the door. The sound of humming approaches. LAO
GAR's *long thin shadow is cast on the patch of sunlight. The shadow*
lowers itself and adopts a squatting position.

TEAM LEADER: Been here seven years, huh?

LAO GAR:* (*Out of shot*) Mm.
> (*The* TEAM LEADER *brings out a packet of cigarettes and*
> *throws it over.* LAO GAR's *hand reaches inside the room, picks*
> *up the cigarettes and withdraws.*)

TEAM LEADER: Got on top of our jobs here?
> (LAO GAR's *shadow moves, and a smoke ring drifts on screen.*)

LAO GAR: (*Out of shot*) Depends on how you look at it. I'll never
be the top hand.

TEAM LEADER: Learned to put up with life in the team?
> (LAO GAR *chuckles.*)
> You've got brains.

LAO GAR: (*Out of shot*) You're the boss. Whatever the job is,
just give me the assignment and I'll do my best.

TEAM LEADER: It's not up to me any more.
> (*He lifts his head and nods towards the tree stump.* LAO GAR
> *reaches inside the room again, and takes the paper from the tree*
> *stump.*)
> When you get there, make a good job of it, eh? Don't let us
> down. You know my third son, learning don't come easy to
> him, try to give him a bit of a prod. Tan his hide if he
> mucks up, you tell me and I'll give him a hiding too.
> (*Still visible,* LAO GAR's *hand folds the paper and withdraws.*

---

*In the main character's name LAO is an honorific prefix, literally meaning 'old';
GAR is his name. GAR means 'pole' or 'rod'.

Out of shot LAO GAR *stands up. A moment later, he tosses the matches back into the room. His shadow reveals that he slowly walks away. The* TEAM LEADER *looks after him and coughs.*)

INT. VILLAGE SHACK. DAY
The shack is used as a dormitory for ZHIQING.*
LAO HEI *is sitting cross-legged on his bed, mending his clothes. Sounds of packing come from offscreen.*
LAO HEI: (*Turning his head*) What the hell are you up to?
LAO GAR: (*Out of shot*) Uh?
   (LAO HEI *hops off the bed and scurries over to the corner.*)
LAO HEI: What's going on?
   (LAO GAR *hands over the paper.*)
   (*Turning the paper this way and that in his hand*) What are you supposed to do?
LAO GAR: Teach.
   (*He picks up a gourd, used as a water bottle, and comes towards the camera, chanting an old poem under his breath.*)
LAO HEI: (*Dumbfounded*) Well, fuck me dead!
   (*A group of* ZHIQING *comes running up the hillside outside the door.*)
ZHIQING: (*Swarming in through the door and talking all at once*) Lao Gar?
   (*They put down their things, run towards the left, twist* LAO GAR's *arms, drag him back into frame and push him down on a bed.*) Go on, tell us, how much did it cost you to buy your way out?
   (LAO HEI, *riding* LAO GAR's *back, screws up the paper and makes as if to throw it away.*)
LI: Are you going to tell us or not? Lao Gar! No? Come on, boys! We'll give his dick a cold bath!
   (*They bring over a large wooden cup. Urging each other on, the* ZHIQING *are about to pour the water.*)
LAO GAR: (*Struggling from a prone position on the bed*) Hold on!
   (*The* ZHIQING *quieten down.*)

---

*Zhiqing is not directly translatable – it's Orwellian Newspeak even in Chinese. It came into use in the Cultural Revolution, specifically to describe young people – mostly former Red Guards – who were relocated from cities to the countryside. They were 'educated' only in so far as they had had basic schooling in the cities.

Any girls around?

ZHIQING: Who cares?

(*The* ZHIQING *start harassing him again.*)

LAO GAR: If I've been hunting round for a cushy job, you can call me a . . .

ZHIQING: What? What? Speak up!

(*They laugh.*)

LAO GAR: (*Embarrassed*) Haha, a . . .

LAO HEI: That's enough, that's enough!

(*The* ZHIQING *fall back, releasing* LAO GAR.)

If he's going to be a teacher, he's got to clean up his language.

(LAO GAR *slowly gets up. He sits on the bed and smooths out the crumpled notification.*)

GIRL: (*Squatting by the stove*) Lao Gar, why do you let them give you such a hard time?

LAO GAR: Everyone's fed up. If it makes them feel better to beat me up, that's fine by me.

WANG: (*Out of shot*) You got to admit Lao Gar's got a good temper . . .

LAO HEI: (*Out of shot*) How come they want you to go and teach?

LAO GAR: How should I know? If you don't believe me, you can go and investigate.

(*The* ZHIQING *disperse and sit on their beds.*)

LAO HEI: Who said anything about investigating? Just don't forget your friends, that's all. If there's a meeting or a movie or something, we go past your school, so we can drop in and get something to drink.

(LAO HEI *puts a milk bottle containing spirits on the ground. The* ZHIQING *get up one by one and toss food on the ground.* WANG *fetches out a hen with its beak tied and tosses it on the ground; he places his hands on the cross beam. The ingredients are in place for a farewell dinner.* ZHANG *leans against the bed and starts to whistle.*)

INT. ZHIQING DORMITORY. DAY

A pair of coarse hands is paring a bamboo tube. A pair of hands takes the bamboo tube, places washed rice inside and pours water in. Beside the fire are two bamboo tubes of rice which have already been cooked. Two green ones hang over the fire. A pair of hands turns them round. There is a hissing noise from the tubes as steam escapes.

INT. ZHIQING DORMITORY. DUSK
Close-up of LAO GAR's *face, flushed with drink.*

LAO GAR: Although I'm going to teach, I'll still have the same kind of life as the rest of you. I won't forget my friends. When you get kids of your own, they'll probably end up in my class, and I won't let your kids down either.

WANG: (*Out of shot*) Why've you got so serious, Lao Gar?

ZHANG: (*Out of shot*) Haven't we all got to know each other pretty well over the last couple of years?

LAIDI: (*Out of shot*) Ah! Boozing away, and no one call your old ma over?
(LAIDI, *a young woman zhiqing with a weight problem, approaches and squats down beside the door, holding a bowl of food in both hands.*)

ZHIQING: Oh, Laidi, come in, come in . . .
(LAIDI *gets up and walks in, swinging her hips.* LAO GAR *is squatting down, his back against the bed.* LAIDI *takes a handful of food and stuffs it in* LAO GAR's *mouth. The* ZHIQING *burst out laughing.* LAIDI *sits on the bed next to* LAO GAR *and stretches her hand to stroke his hair, which is standing on end.*)

LAIDI: (*Swaying her top half*) So you're off to be a teacher! I'm going to miss you!

WANG: (*Out of shot*) Why not go a bit lower down while you're at it? Gently!
(LAO GAR *grips* LAIDI's *fat hand and flings it away vigorously.*)

LAIDI: Hey . . .
(*The* ZHIQING *roar with laughter.*)

LAO HEI: It's only when he's leaving that you're getting soft on him. I reckon you wouldn't mind a transfer too – work as a cook on a fat school salary.

LAIDI: Lao Hei! Stop picking on your old ma! You're making a big mistake if you think I only know how to cook. I can read music, I can sing – how about that! So why can't I go and teach music? (*She claps* LAO GAR *on the shoulder.*) Lao

69

Gar, you know your old ma's got loads of talent, don't you?

LAO GAR: Yes, yes.

LAIDI: When you get to the school, ask if there's a chance for me. I just need a score and I'll have the whole school singing in less than an hour.

(*The* ZHIQING *laugh.* LAIDI *pours some spirits from a bottle into a coarse earthenware bowl, tilts her head back and finishes it off. She rests the bottle on her leg.*)

Good stuff!

(*The* ZHIQING *cheer.*)

Do this for your old ma, Lao Gar, and I'll finish off the bottle in your honour!

(LAIDI *is about to pour herself some more.*)

LAO HEI: Hang on! That's other people's grog you're polishing off!

LAIDI: What's so precious about this dog's piss? Call yourselves men and you're not even halfway down the bottle yet! No girl'd ever go for any of you lot!

LAO HEI: No one'd ever make you an offer, anyway!

(LAIDI *puts down the bottle and pushes* LAO HEI *to the ground. The* ZHIQING *roar with laughter.*)

INT. ZHIQING DORMITORY. NIGHT

Camera pans over Chinese chess pieces. LAO GAR, *drunk, mutters to nobody in particular. A commotion: someone spots a lizard. Light out – blackout.*

EXT. THE RIVER BANK. MORNING MIST

LAO GAR *and* LAO HEI *wade across the river, bags on their shoulders, water dripping from their bodies.*

ZHIQING: (*Out of shot*) Taking your machete to the school? Hadn't you better throw it away and try to look like a teacher?

(*Out of shot the* ZHIQING *laugh.* LAO GAR *vigorously slices at the water with a long bamboo stick in his hand.*)

ZHIQING: (*Out of shot*) That's right! Give the kids a whack when they muck up!

(LAO GAR *and* LAO HEI *climb the bank and walk to the left.*)

GIRL ZHIQING: (*Out of shot*) Hey! Walk properly!

(*Sporadic laughter offscreen.*)

EXT. THE MOUNTAIN FOREST. MORNING MIST
A misty, mysterious mountain forest. The sound of offscreen laughter fades, and is replaced by the sounds of tree-felling, echoing in the mist.

EXT. A PATH IN THE FOREST. MORNING MIST
Seen from behind, LAO GAR *and* LAO HEI *appear on screen walking downhill into the forest. Tree-felling, birdsong offscreen.*

EXT. A MOUNTAIN GULLY. MORNING MIST
In the background is the vegetation of a primordial forest. To the right is a huge dead tree. Above the tree, framed between two mountains, appears a puff of smoke. LAO GAR *and* LAO HEI *walk forward from deep in the forest. They pause for a moment and gaze ahead. They turn and walk away.*

EXT. A MOUNTAINSIDE. MORNING MIST
In the background is a shining river. Seen from behind, LAO GAR *and* LAO HEI *walk downhill.*

EXT. ON THE MOUNTAINSIDE. MORNING MIST
Gigantic tree roots hang over the slope, the roots twisted and intertwined, still stained with red earth. LAO GAR *and* LAO HEI, *skirting the roots, make their way downhill with difficulty.*

EXT. A STEEP CLIFF. MORNING MIST
From above, we see a steep cliff face entirely bare of vegetation, showing eroded red earth.

EXT. A MOUNTAINSIDE. MORNING MIST
LAO GAR *and* LAO HEI *stop, dumbstruck, and stare ahead. The sound of a large tree falling, out of shot. After a pause,* LAO HEI *turns and walks away.* LAO GAR *follows, turning his head back to look.*

EXT. EASTER ISLAND. MORNING MIST
The mountainside is covered with blackened tree stumps, which in the mist seem to have human shapes. The vegetation at the foot of

the stumps is sparse. The atmosphere is eerie, like a kind of Easter Island. LAO GAR *and* LAO HEI *make their way through the tree stumps towards the left. Music.*

EXT. A PATH. MORNING MIST
A herd of cattle emerges through the mist. Seen from behind LAO GAR *and* LAO HEI *emerge from the right and walk towards the cattle. Behind the cattle, dressed in white clothes and his face screened by a battered straw hat, a* COWHERD *slowly walks along, waving a bamboo stick. The misty, mysterious mountain forest. Seen from behind, the* COWHERD *walks offscreen.* LAO GAR *and* LAO HEI *pause as they catch sight of their destination.*

EXT. LOOKING DOWN FROM A MOUNTAINSIDE AT THE SCHOOL. MORNING MIST
The thatched huts in the background are concealed by the mist. Seen from behind, LAO GAR *and* LAO HEI *walk along the red path.*

EXT. SCHOOL YARD. MORNING MIST
LAO GAR *and* LAO HEI *come up the hillside.* LAO GAR *weighs his machete in his hand. Out of shot a* MALE TEACHER *can be heard giving a class.*
LAO HEI: (*Offering* LAO GAR *a cigarette*) What're you doing? Trying to kill someone?

INT. SCHOOL OFFICE. DARK
CHEN, *the headmaster, is standing at the side of his desk, shaking a clock. Two* FEMALE TEACHERS *are sitting to the left preparing lessons.*

EXT. SCHOOL YARD. MORNING MIST
A dead tree in the mist. A piece of iron, which serves as the school gong, hangs from the tree.

INT. SCHOOL OFFICE. DARK
The office door is pushed open. CHEN *turns his head. The* FEMALE TEACHERS *lift their heads.*
CHEN: (*Out of shot*) Come in, come in!
   (LAO HEI *leans against the doorway. Seen from behind,* CHEN *stretches out his hand to him.* LAO HEI *withdraws his hand, rubs his neck and grins.* LAO GAR *dodges out from behind* LAO HEI *and hands over a piece of crumpled paper.*)
   (*Out of shot*) Oh, it's you!
   (LAO HEI *cackles. From offscreen comes the noise of* CHILDREN *playing.*)

EXT. SCHOOL YARD. MORNING MIST
The CHILDREN *rush out from the classrooms, chasing each other and shouting. They play ball games, skipping and so on.*

INT. SCHOOL OFFICE. DARK
LAO GAR: (*Sitting on a bench, clutching his machete*) I only did one year at senior high before coming here. I've never taught before. I'm not sure that I can.
CHEN: Here, have some water.
   (LAO GAR *gets up to take the water and drops the machete. By the door, some* CHILDREN *suddenly poke their heads in.*)
CHILDREN: Beanpole, ha ha . . .

(LAO HEI *enters the shot and crosses to chase away the* CHILDREN.)

CHEN: You can put your machete on the table. Here, on the table.

(LAO GAR, *seen from behind in the foreground, places his machete on the desk. A* FEMALE TEACHER *in the background looks at* LAO GAR *in surprise. The machete on the desk vibrates, gleaming white. Seen from behind,* LAO GAR *sits down slowly. The* FEMALE TEACHER *lowers her head.*)

EXT. SCHOOL YARD. MORNING MIST

The CHILDREN *are playing in the yard. At the sound of the gong, they make their way towards the classrooms, playing up and chasing each other.* LAO HEI *walks towards the school office. The camera pans slowly right as* LAO GAR *comes out of Chen's office, following* CHEN.

INT. LAO GAR'S ROOM. DARK

CHEN *opens the door and goes in. The silhouettes of* LAO GAR *and* LAO HEI *are outlined in the doorway. Inside the hut it is very dark. Waste paper scattered over the earth floor catches the light.*

CHEN: (*Going inside*) This is where you sleep. There's a bed . . .

(LAO HEI *and* LAO GAR *lean against the doorway.*)

(*Out of shot*) . . . and here's the desk.

LAO HEI: (*Lifting his head to look at the roof*) Well, fuck me.

(CHEN *stands by the west window.* LAO HEI *pushes* CHEN *aside, opens the window and looks out.*)

EXT. LAO GAR'S ROOM. DARK

Seen through the west window from outside, LAO GAR, *wiping away his sweat, comes over to the window, sits down and looks outside.* LAO HEI *walks past outside, throwing a bundle of straw on the ground.*

LAO GAR: (*Lifting his gourd and taking a mouthful of water*) Lao Hei, next time you come, bring my hoe with you.

LAO HEI: (*Out of shot*) I thought you'd have it easy here!

LAO GAR: We're all stuck here! Who has it easy?

LAO HEI: (*Out of shot*) So it's not such a cushy job after all.

(*Smoke rises from a fire offscreen.* LAO GAR *gazes out dumbly as the smoke drifts past his face.*)

INT. LAO GAR'S ROOM. DARK

The room has been tidied up and the sticks holding up the bamboo blinds over the windows have been set up. In the middle of the room there is a tree stump which serves as a chopping block. LAO GAR *and* LAO HEI *look around.*

LAO GAR: Fine, excellent. (*Discovering the word* BASTARD *on* LAO HEI*'s arm*) Ah! Ha ha!

LAO HEI: Shit!

(*He brushes it off, looking outside the door, right.* LAO GAR *and* LAO HEI *light cigarettes, and* LAO HEI *hoists himself up on to the bamboo desk.* LAO GAR *sits on a chair. Suddenly, the chair collapses and he tumbles to the ground.* LAO HEI, *perched on the desk, starts laughing. The desk suddenly collapses and* LAO HEI *is sent sprawling on to the ground.*)

Ouch!

(*He tries to get up.* LAO GAR *helps* LAO HEI *up.*)

Bloody kids . . .

(LAO GAR *and* LAO HEI *go over to the bed, and cautiously sit down to try it out. When they are safely seated, they relax and rock the bed frame, laughing.*)

INT. SCHOOL OFFICE. DAY

LAO GAR *takes up a cane and tucks it under his arm. He picks up the textbook and shakes it. Out falls a leaf specimen; a cloud of chalk dust also flies out.*

LAO GAR: (*Picking up the leaf*) Who did this book belong to before? He wasn't suffering from some disease, was he?

(CHEN, *coming onscreen left, goes up to the desk.*)

FEMALE TEACHER: (*Out of shot*) Yes, of course he was, ha ha . . .

LAO GAR: (*Abruptly dropping the book*) What disease?

CHEN: (*Bending over to pick up the book*) Ah, what's all this about diseases? Mr Li, the teacher who left, was a bit careless, that's all. But he never lost the book, and that's something.

(CHEN *gives the textbook to* LAO GAR *and moves out of shot.*)

Best you don't lose it either, because if you do, it won't be easy to find another.

(*He picks up a set square and moves back in shot.*)

(*Handing* LAO GAR *a sheet of paper*) Oh yes, here's the timetable.

LAO GAR: (*Takes it, then looks up.*) The third-year class?

EXT. SCHOOL YARD. DAY

LAO GAR *and* CHEN *walk towards the classrooms.*

LAO GAR: Ah, how far have they got?

CHEN: Term's just started. Probably still Lesson One. Or maybe Lesson Two!

(CHEN *goes into the classroom.* LAO GAR *stands outside under the eaves, hesitating. Seen from outside,* LAO GAR*'s face is hidden by the thatch, and all we can see is a hand holding the chalk, the cane and the textbook. From offscreen comes the noise of the* CHILDREN *playing up.*)

(*Out of shot*) Today, there's a new teacher . . .

(*Seen from behind,* LAO GAR *is standing under the eaves, shuffling his feet uneasily. The classroom is very noisy.*)

(*Seen from the outside*) Quiet!

(*Out of shot*) Anyone fooling around is going to catch it! (*Pause.*) Today, there's a new teacher coming to take you. Now mind you pay attention.

(*As before,* LAO GAR *is standing under the eaves.* CHEN, *moving into shot, passes by* LAO GAR *and goes straight off. Looking as if he would like to go back too,* LAO GAR *drops the box of chalk, hastily picks it up and ducks under the eaves. The hubbub subsides.*)

INT. THIRD-YEAR CLASSROOM. DAY

Seen from the back of the room, LAO GAR *comes in from outside.*

MONITOR: Stand up!

(*One by one the* CHILDREN *stand up.*)

BOY: (*Mischievously*) Sit down!

(*The* CHILDREN *sit down again.*)

BOY A: (*Turning around*) Why does everyone sit down before the teacher tells us to?

(*Seen from behind, the* CHILDREN *stand up again.*)

LAO GAR: Let's begin.

(*He goes up to the teacher's platform.* BOY B *rolls a pencil on his upper lip. After a moment the pencil drops and the* BOY *laughs.* LAO GAR *looks up, startled.* GIRL A, *looking*

dissatisfied, puts her head to one side. BOY C *rubs his ear.* GIRL
B *stares straight ahead. The* CHILDREN, *standing with their
hands behind their backs, look doubtfully at the platform.*)
Er, let's begin. (*Pause.*) Oh, sit down!
(*Out of shot, the* CHILDREN *sit down with a sigh.*)
What lesson are you up to?
CHILDREN: (*Out of shot, all at once.*) Lesson One . . . It should
be Lesson Two.
LAO GAR: (*Lowering his head*) All right. Turn to page 4.
(*Out of shot, the sound of talking.*)
Turn to page 4.
(*Out of shot, the sound of suppressed giggling.*)
Turn to page 4, everyone.
(*Out of shot, the giggling gets louder.*)
(*With a note of irritation, pointing at the front row*) You there!
Where's your book?
BOY A: What book? We don't have any books!
LAO GAR: Who's the class monitor?
(*Seen from behind, in the foreground, the* MONITOR *timidly
stands up. Her features are more delicate than most of the other
children's.*)
Are you the class monitor?
(*She nods.*)
Tell me, what's the point in coming to class if you don't
bring your books?
(*Pause.*)
MONITOR: There aren't any books.
LAO GAR: There aren't any? Then what do you do in class?
MONITOR: (*Seen front on, together with some of the* CHILDREN)
Every lesson, Mr Zhang, then it was Mr Li, they'd copy
out the lesson on the blackboard. They'd teach the bit
they'd copied out, and we'd copy it down in our exercise
books.
LAO GAR: (*Out of shot*) Didn't the school issue books to you?
(*The* MONITOR *shakes her head.*)
(*Out of shot*) None at all?
(*As before, the* MONITOR *shakes her head. Seen from behind,
the* CHILDREN *whisper to each other; the classroom gets very
noisy.*)
(*In the background*) All right!

(*The noise subsides.*)
Officials without seals and students without books. Is going to school just a kind of game then? When I went to school . . .
(*He talks to the blackboard and stands side on. On the blackboard is a caricature of* LAO GAR, *labelled with his name:* THIS IS LAO GAR! LAO GAR *looks at the blackboard, then turns around, embarrassed.*)
Er, when I went to school, on the first day of term, the first thing books were issued, all brand new, and you'd make dust jackets for them. I'd bring them to school every day, and each class I'd bring out the books for that class . . .
(*Suddenly he breaks off and lifts his head. From offscreen comes the sound of a* FEMALE TEACHER *in the next classroom. Seen from behind, the* CHILDREN *are sitting upright, silent.* LAO GAR *stands there blankly for a moment, hastily goes outside, then turns and comes back in.*)
(*Waving his hand at the* MONITOR) Sit down.

(She sits down. LAO GAR goes out through the door. The CHILDREN stare after him talking quietly among themselves. WANG FU lowers his head and takes up a pencil.)

INT. SCHOOL OFFICE. DAY
CHEN is sitting trimming his nails by the light from the skylight. To the left, two FEMALE TEACHERS are correcting homework. LAO GAR enters right.

CHEN: *(Looking up)* Oh, did you forget something?

LAO GAR: It's not me, the school's forgotten to issue books to the students.

CHEN: Oh, I forgot to tell you. There aren't any books. We haven't issued any for the last few years. There's a paper shortage.
(LAO GAR goes over to the wall where there is a high stack of printed government papers. He riffles through the top few.)
Help yourself. They're good for papering your walls. You can also wipe your bum on them.
(The FEMALE TEACHERS titter.)
Er, shouldn't say things like that, shouldn't say things like that.
(LAO GAR puts the papers back, straightens the pile, turns and goes out of the door.)

EXT. SCHOOL YARD. DAY
Seen from inside the classroom, LAO GAR hurries across.

INT. THIRD-YEAR CLASSROOM. DAY
The CHILDREN look right, expectantly. From offscreen comes the sound of footsteps. Cut to the caricature of LAO GAR on the blackboard. LAO GAR stands sideways in front of the teacher's desk, smiling apologetically. Cut to the caricature of LAO GAR. LAO GAR, moving into shot left, looks at the blackboard and wipes it clean with the duster. The classroom suddenly gets noisy as the CHILDREN take out their books and pencils. Seen from behind, LAO GAR writes out the lesson. The CHILDREN sit upright at their desks, getting ready to copy. Seen from behind, LAO GAR copies the lesson from the textbook.

INT. THIRD-YEAR CLASSROOM. DARK AND MISTY
The CHILDREN *are copying the lesson, occasionally lifting their eyes and looking front. A* BOY *in the back row rises and stretches. Seen from behind,* LAO GAR *chalks up the lesson. He has reached Lesson Three. The* MONITOR *is writing rapidly. She lifts her head for a moment, puts down her pencil and, cupping her chin in her hand, looks offscreen right.*

EXT. SCHOOL YARD. DARK AND MISTY
Seen from inside the classroom: the empty door and the damp red earth. In the background, faintly visible through the mist, is a gnarled tree stump.

INT. THIRD-YEAR CLASSROOM. NIGHT
A large number of oil lamps are glowing brightly in the classroom. By their light the CHILDREN *are industriously copying, from time to time lifting their heads.* LAO GAR *is leaning against the doorway, holding a lamp in his right hand, looking through the textbook. After a moment, he lifts his head.* BOY D *sits blankly, exhausted.* BOY C *pushes his pencil against his lip.* GIRL C *stares ahead.* BOY F *lifts a bamboo ring as if measuring something. The oil lamps flicker in the empty classroom. Alone,* LAO GAR *stands on the platform. Confused and exhausted, he blows out the lamp in his hand.*

INT. THIRD-YEAR CLASSROOM. DUSK
LAO GAR, *exhausted, wipes off the blackboard. The* CHILDREN *run out of the door.* LAO GAR *wearily turns round and props himself on the teacher's desk, covered in chalk dust. In long shot, from the back of the room, he realizes that one boy is still at his desk.* LAO GAR *looks at him quizzically. The* BOY, WANG FU, *gathers up his things, slings a large wicker basket over his shoulder and crosses the room, picking his way through the desks. He climbs over the classroom's low partition wall and leaves.* LAO GAR *stands alone at his desk.*

EXT. THIRD-YEAR CLASSROOM. DUSK
Through the doorway of the classroom. A football lies, untouched.

EXT. SCHOOL YARD. DUSK
LAO GAR *tests the weight of the huge stone roller in the school yard.*

EXT. SCHOOL YARD. DUSK
LAO GAR *wanders through the deserted classrooms and out the back.*
He is following a sound he has heard.

EXT. CLEARING. DUSK
A WOODSMAN *serves tea to* LAO GAR *in a clearing. He starts to*
sing.

EXT. CLEARING. DUSK
The WOODSMAN'S *song, apparently not in Chinese, carries over.*
The WOODSMAN *sits in his hut singing. Light streams in through*
bamboo slats behind him. LAO GAR *sits listening, cross-legged.*
Then, LAO GAR *bursts into laughter and runs off.*

EXT. HILLSIDE. DUSK
Still laughing aloud, LAO GAR *runs back up the hill towards the*
school. He pauses to take in the sounds around him, which well up
on the soundtrack: cowbells, cries, a distant song.

INT. LAO GAR'S ROOM. NIGHT
At first it is completely dark. After a moment, LAO GAR *strikes a match and lights the lamp. He lifts his head. On the bamboo wall two broken pieces of mirror hang side by side. The lamplight sways and flickers in the mirror. Carrying the lamp in both hands,* LAO GAR *slowly approaches. We can see his reflection in the mirror, the image of his face split into two.* LAO GAR *purses his lips and puffs. Suddenly a drop of spittle flies from offscreen and lands on the reflection of the face in the mirror.*

EXT. CLEARING. DAY
A herd of cattle loiters.

INT. THIRD-YEAR CLASSROOM. DAY
Seen from behind, LAO GAR *is copying a new lesson on the blackboard. From offscreen comes the voice of a* FEMALE TEACHER *next door, which continues over the next few scenes. In the foreground the* CHILDREN *copy the lesson. In the background, the* COWHERD *is in the side classroom. He turns round and takes a piece of chalk.* LAO GAR *stops copying and turns his head. The* COWHERD *looks at something on the blackboard in the side classroom. In the foreground, one of the* CHILDREN *turns his head and looks.* LAO GAR *turns back to the blackboard and continues copying. The third-year classroom, seen from the side classroom: the sound of the chalk stops. After a pause,* LAO GAR *comes out of the classroom and, walking under the eaves, goes up to the bamboo fence around the side classroom.* WANG FU *turns his head. From offscreen comes the sound of the cattle being shooed on, which continues over the next few scenes.* LAO GAR *turns his head and looks.*

EXT. CLEARING. DAY
The COWHERD *walks away, shooing the cattle and brandishing a bamboo switch at them.*

INT. SIDE CLASSROOM. DAY
A handful of mud has been thrown on a chalk drawing of concentric circles in the middle of the blackboard, with leaves, grass and flowers sticking out, swaying lightly.

INT. THIRD-YEAR CLASSROOM. DAY

The third-year classroom, seen from side on and incorporating some of the red-earth clearing. Coming in right, LAO GAR *gazes towards the left, and after a moment walks quickly into the classroom. Inside the classroom we hear the noise of chalk writing fast. A moment later, the sound of the chalk stops, and* LAO GAR *walks out of the classroom, gazes to the left and quickly walks out of shot. The voice of the* FEMALE TEACHER *next door has stopped. Music starts: The sound of a* suona.*

INT. THIRD-YEAR CLASSROOM. DAY

From outside we see the dim figures of the CHILDREN *inside the bamboo fence.*

BOY: Finished, sir!

(*From the front we see the* CHILDREN *looking to the right, sitting upright with their hands behind their backs.*)

LAO GAR: (*Seen from behind, coming into shot right*) Everyone finished?

CHILDREN: (*Singing out in turn*) Finished! Finished . . .

LAO GAR: (*Seen face on*) You've finished copying, but do you understand what it says?

(*The* CHILDREN *whisper among themselves.*)

The lesson is very simple: it's a story about a village.

(*Pauses, and points to a student.*) Er, you! Tell us what it's about.

(*Seen from behind, the* BOY *looks to right and left and then stands up irresolutely.* WANG FU, *looking intently.*)

BOY: (*Seen from behind, stretching his head forwards and looking at the blackboard*) I don't know.

(*He sits down.*)

LAO GAR: On your feet! What do you mean, you don't know? It's easy enough. You're not dumb!

BOY: (*Seen face on, standing up*) If I did know, what would we need you to teach us for?

(*Turning around, he tosses his head and sits down again. The* CHILDREN *cheer their agreement.* WANG FU *frowns.*)

LAO GAR: (*Pointing at the* MONITOR) You!

(*The* MONITOR *looks up and makes to stand up.*)

A suona *is a Chinese brass instrument.*

(*Holding the cane*) In simple words, a village landlord engaging in sabotage is exposed by the poor and lower-middle peasants. Afterwards, production in this village increases.

(*The* MONITOR, *seen from behind, timidly stands up.*)

You need me to teach you this? Speak up!

MONITOR: (*Eyes turned upwards*) In simple words, a village landlord engaging in sabotage was – um, *is* exposed by the poor and lower-middle peasants. Afterwards, production in that – um, no, afterwards production in *this* village increases.

(LAO GAR *listens, dumbfounded.*)

(*Smiling complacently*) Did I do it right, sir?

BOY: (*Affectedly*) Yes!

(*The* CHILDREN *giggle.*)

LAO GAR: (*Seen from behind*) You've got a good memory.

WANG FU: (*At the back of the room, screened off by the other* CHILDREN) You're not much of a teacher.

(*The other* CHILDREN *quickly turn their heads.*)

Why don't you teach like you're supposed to? First you give us the new words, then you divide it into paragraphs, then you give the main idea of each paragraph, then you give us the writing style. Even I could teach this. I bet your work in the team was lousy. You only came here to have it a bit easier!

(WANG FU *stands up.* LAO GAR *is stunned. Suddenly he smiles.* WANG FU *extends his hand and scratches his chin. Suddenly from offscreen comes the sound of another class singing, which continues until the end of the scene. Close-up of* LAO GAR's *smiling face.* WANG FU *stands stubbornly during the singing.*)

EXT. SCHOOL YARD. DAY

As the singing continues, the CHILDREN *rush out of the classroom to play, pushing and shoving. The song, one currently being promoted by the authorities, sounds like people quarrelling although the words cannot be distinguished.* LAO GAR *and* CHEN *emerge from their respective classrooms and are pushed this way and that by the children playing.*

84

EXT. SCHOOL YARD. DUSK

The light from the setting sun covers the teachers' rooms. The thatched hut and dead tree appear silhouetted against the sky. LAO GAR, *squatting, looks like a black stone. After a moment, he stands up, pulls closer the shirt sleeves draped around his shoulders, then swings his body so that the two empty sleeves flap like arms. The sound of wild singing comes from afar.*

INT. THIRD-YEAR CLASSROOM. DUSK

LAO GAR: (*Moving left*) You should have learned the character for 'life' ages ago. What does 'life' mean? It means living. To live you have to eat and drink, so the character for 'living' is written with the character for 'water' on the left and the character for 'tongue' on the right.

EXT. SCHOOL YARD. DUSK

Dark clouds hang over the mountains. LAO GAR *stands silently in front of the huts rubbing his arms. The sound of native singing approaches then recedes.*

INT. THIRD-YEAR CLASSROOM. DAY

The seated CHILDREN *are seen front on.* LAO GAR, *seen from behind, enters the classroom carrying his teaching materials.*

MONITOR: Stand up!

    (*The* CHILDREN *stand up.* LAO GAR *bows very earnestly to the* CHILDREN. *The* CHILDREN *remain standing, whispering among themselves in surprise.* LAO GAR *bows again. The* CHILDREN *giggle.*)

LAO GAR: Sit down!

    (*The* CHILDREN *sit down, still whispering.*)

    Wang Fu!

WANG FU: (*Out of shot*) Present!

    (*From offscreen comes the faint sound of the* FEMALE TEACHER *and the* CHILDREN *next door reading the textbook.*)

LAO GAR: (*Hesitating*) Er, first I should mention something. You don't have to bother any more with this standing up in class. What's the point in standing up if you don't have any books? Another thing, you don't have to put your hands behind your back in class. You can talk, and you can leave your seat if you have to. You've all grown up in the

mountains, and now you're in your last year in school.
(*The* CHILDREN *relax, put their hands on the desks and become active. In the background, a lesson is taking place in the side classroom.*)
Wang Fu!
(WANG FU, *in one of the back rows, gets up.*)
You can speak sitting down.
(WANG FU, *remaining on his feet, looks at* LAO GAR. LAO GAR *walks over to* WANG FU, *presses him down in his seat and turns round.*)
Wang Fu, you said you could teach. Well, come and show me how to teach.

WANG FU: (*Standing up sharply*) Do you want to punish me?
(*Seen from behind,* LAO GAR *stops, dumbfounded. He turns his head and looks at* WANG FU. *The indistinct sound of the class next door is interrupted.*)

LAO GAR: (*Turning round*) No. (*Walks forward.*) I've only just got to the school, and I only got the textbook just before starting. To be frank, I know how to read fairly well, but I've never taught before. I don't know the best way to teach you. Tell me how Mr Zhang and Mr Li used to teach.
(WANG FU *lowers his head uneasily. The sound of teaching next door becomes indistinct again.*)
Come up here in front of the blackboard and show me which words you don't know. I don't know how much you can read. Come on!
(WANG FU, *moving into shot, walks up to the blackboard.*)
Underline all the words you don't know.
(WANG FU *takes the piece of chalk. Seen from behind,* WANG FU, *holding the chalk, hesitates in front of the blackboard. He underlines several characters. One of them is a character that does not exist in Chinese: a combination of the characters for 'Cattle' and 'Water', by which* LAO GAR *means 'Cattlepiss'. Finished,* WANG FU *leaves the blackboard.* LAO GAR *slightly embarrassed, goes to the blackboard, rubs out the invented character, and turns around.*)
All right, I'll explain all the words underlined.

CHILDREN: (*Out of shot, clamouring*) Sir, there's some other words we don't know.

LAO GAR: All right . . . (*Waving his hand*) Everyone up to the
blackboard!
(*Several* CHILDREN *race up, draw their lines and then run
back to their seats.* LAO GAR *looks at the blackboard, on which
most words are now underlined, turns around and suddenly
laughs. The* CHILDREN *also burst out laughing.*)
No wonder you don't know what the lesson means.
Actually, you should have learned at least half of these
words in primary school.
WANG FU: (*Standing up*) Sir, the two words I underlined we've
never had before. I can prove it to you.
LAO GAR: OK. First I'll explain all the underlined words. Then
we'll go through the real new words more slowly.
CHILDREN: Yessir!

EXT. UNDER THE CLASSROOM EAVES. DAY
The CHILDREN *rush out from the classroom, hopping over the*
bamboo railing, and scatter in all directions.
LAO GAR: (*Coming out through the door, shaking the chalk-covered*
   duster) Wang Fu!
   (*After a pause,* WANG FU *steps forward timidly.* LAO GAR *goes*
   into the classroom, puts down the duster and comes out again.)
   Wang Fu, you said you could prove which words really
   were new. How can you do that?
   (WANG FU *quickly goes into the classroom. Inside the classroom*
   WANG FU *comes to the window.* LAO GAR, *still outside,*
   approaches him.)
WANG FU: (*Handing over a red notebook*) Here, look.
   (LAO GAR *turns around and squats down against the wall,*
   opening the book.)
   'Presented to . . .' Are you Wang Qitong's son? (*He gets up*
   and sits sideways on the railing.) I know your father, once we

loaded rice together. Your father's very strong, but he's not much of a talker. So, Wang Qitong's son . . .
(*He gets down and squats against the wall.* WANG FU, *a little embarrassed, sits inside the wall leaning over the railing.* LAO GAR *leafs through the notebook. It is full of characters written very neatly in columns. He lifts up a botanical specimen pressed inside the book, looks at it, then turns to another page. Seen from the yard,* LAO GAR *and* WANG FU *sit facing each other, both inside the classroom.*)

EXT. SCHOOL YARD. DUSK
The setting sun gleams, and smoke from the cookhouse curls upwards. WANG FU *passes by the millstone and goes downhill.*

EXT. SCHOOL YARD. MORNING MIST
LAO GAR, *his satchel and straw hat hanging from his shoulder, squats on a bench, smoking.* CHEN *moves into shot, goes up to a chair and picks up the soap.*
CHEN: Ah, correcting their homework's really an effort. You have to guess half the words. Sometimes I'm up till midnight trying to make some of them out.
(LAO GAR *chuckles.*)
(*Moving out of shot*) Oh, aren't your classes the same?
LAO GAR: We're all under the same headmaster, aren't we? How could they be any different?
CHEN: (*Appearing in shot lathering his face*) You shouldn't say things like that. (*Goes up to the chair and picks up a towel.*) You're teaching reading and writing, it isn't the same as teaching maths. But how to divide into paragraphs (*moves out of shot*), give the main idea of each paragraph, the overall theme and so on, there's standard rules for all that! The school in town's got a teachers' book with all the standard rules. If you like I can tell you how to get there, and you can go and make a copy.
(LAO GAR *laughs, gets down from the bench and walks out of shot.*)
(*Out of shot*) Eh?
(*On screen only the vast mist remains bordering the red earth, setting off the chair and the bench.*)

INT. ZHIQING DORMITORY. DUSK

LAO HEI *and* WANG *are noisily playing the finger-guessing game and drinking.* LAO GAR *and the* TEAM LEADER *are drinking and chatting at their leisure.*

TEAM LEADER: . . . that boy of mine, he wrote a letter to the folks back home, and three days later we got a reply. I told him to read it out to me, but he stuttered and stammered so much I couldn't make head nor tail of it, nor him either.

(LAO HEI *stops the finger-guessing game and squats down.*)

LAO HEI: Still on about that letter, are you? Wonder you're not ashamed to bring it up. Afterwards, he got me to read it for him. I tried, but I couldn't make any sense of it. Then I asked him whose grandad he was. He said he wasn't anyone's grandad, so when I told him the letter was addressed to a grandad, he started rubbing his head. Finally, I figured it out. It was actually the letter his son had written, returned to sender. He'd been pretending it was the reply he was reading out.

(*The* ZHIQING *burst out laughing.*)

The receiver's address and the sender's address were written the wrong way round. The writing looked like a bunch of crabs. I nearly bit my tongue off trying to read it out.

TEAM LEADER: Ah, a bad business. (*To* LAO GAR) I hear you're taking the third-year class?

(LAO GAR *nods.*)

Now that's really something! If you finished primary school, in the old days you'd be called a County Scholar, and a Provincial Graduate if you did junior high. A Provincial Graduate was really something: everyone'd make up to them! (*To the* ZHIQING) He's teaching Provincial Graduates, that's really something!

LAO GAR: Your son'll be a Provincial Graduate one day.

TEAM LEADER: No, how could he ever reach that high?

(*The* ZHIQING *laugh.*)

LAO GAR: (*Relaxing*) It's better here in the team, it's not so lonely.

ZHANG: (*Cynically*) What, aren't there women teachers at the school?

(*One of the girls hits* ZHANG, *who covers his mouth and sniggers.*)

GIRL: (*Out of shot*) You prick!

LAO GAR: There's some educated people from somewhere or other, but there's not a sound from them after dark.
(*He gets up and stretches out on the bed, only his legs remaining on screen.* LAO HEI's *plump hand pats* LAO GAR's *leg.*)

LAIDI: (*Standing in the doorway*) What sort of sounds do you want to hear after work?
(*She strolls over and sits on the bed beside* LAO HEI.)

LAO HEI: There's not enough room for three on my bed.
(LAIDI *gives* LAO HEI *a shove; he retreats to the other side and sits on the ground.* LAO GAR *sits up.*)

LAIDI: Piss off then, so I can have a nice chat with our teacher.
(*She stretches out her hand and strokes* LAO GAR's *fface.*) Ah, you must be teaching indoors all the time, look how pale you've got.

LAO GAR: (*Brushing* LAIDI's *plump hand aside*) Keep your hands to yourself!

LAIDI: (*Hands in her lap*) Putting on airs, now, are we? The masses have to keep our distance! Let me tell you something, even if you taught for a hundred years, you think your old ma doesn't know what you've got dangling between your legs? Huh! Only a few days and he's pretending to be a gentleman, squeezing his legs together!

LAO GAR: (*Squatting down against the bed*) Who's squeezing?
(*The* ZHIQING *laugh.*)
There's a boy in my class, Wang Fu, who knows 3,888 characters. He gave me a hard time the first few lessons. Afterwards, it was him that taught me how to teach.
(*The* ZHIQING *look at each other.*)

ZHANG: (*To* LAO HEI) How many characters do you know?

LAO HEI: I tell people I finished junior high, but in fact I never even finished primary school. How many bloody characters do you think I'd know?
(*The* TEAM LEADER's *puzzled face.*)

BOY: Hey, how many characters do you know?

BOY 2: Me? Ha ha . . .

LAO GAR: When I was at school we had a junior teacher. He lived at home with his mother, who used to assemble

91

matchboxes, forty-six cents a thousand, to send him to school. Afterwards, the poor bastard stayed on as a teacher after he got through school – his marks had been pretty good. But because he looked a bit rough round the edges, and he was fairly young, he hadn't any control over the students. Then one day he said, 'I don't know how good you are at your other subjects, but let's just take reading and writing. See this dictionary: open it at random, any page, and if you've got – well, if there aren't any characters on that page that you can't write, or explain, or read, I'll give in: I won't bother any more when you fool around in class.' The kids didn't believe him: right away they picked up the dictionary, opened it and looked at the page – ha ha, they all gave in – not a single one of them knew all the characters on the page.

(*The* ZHIQING *look at each other.*)

ZHANG: Who's got a dictionary?

(*They all say that they don't have one.*)

LAO GAR: I don't either. Whoever thought of bringing a dictionary with us when we came here?

LAIDI: (*Sitting with her arms clasped around her knees*) How can you be 'King of the Children' without a dictionary? Never mind. Your old ma's got one.

LAO GAR: Bring it over then.

LAIDI: I'll bring it over on one condition.

(*She stands up.* LAO GAR *cranes his neck to look at her.*)
We don't want to be a team leader, *we* don't want to be a team official, *we* just want to be a music teacher: what about it? Isn't a dictionary worth a teaching job? Seeing that the real teacher doesn't even have one!

(*She goes to the door. During her speech the* ZHIQING *giggle.*)

LAO GAR: What's so special about a dictionary? I can go and buy one.

LAIDI: Where? There's none in the county town. Are you going off to the provincial capital? (*Moving out of shot*) Ask your class who's got a dictionary!

(*The* TEAM LEADER *squats by the side of a bed, smoking his water pipe.*)

LAIDI: (*Out of shot*) Lao Gar, go back and tell the school, tell them there's a Laidi in our team who's got so many songs

92

she doesn't know what to do with them. They can ask her to go and teach some of them.

LAO GAR: (*Out of shot*) I'm not the boss, how can I get a transfer for you?

LAIDI: How about this? You write the words and I'll write the music. Then you teach our song to the kids in your class. It'll be something really different. Then when the leaders ask about it, tell them it was written by Laidi from our team. Once the leaders know how good I am, I bet they'll ask me to come and teach music.

(*Out of shot, the* ZHIQING *burst out laughing.* LAO GAR *gets up, walks to the door and moves out of shot.*)

LAO HEI: (*In the foreground*) Write music? You think that's some kind of joke? It's art, you got to make a special study of it, at the very least you've got to go to university. You're crazy, you're out of your mind!

(*The* ZHIQING *laugh.*)

LAIDI: What's so difficult about it . . .

(*Out of shot, one of the others hums a tune.*)

Shut up! . . . Those things I'm always humming, I just need to write them down and that's music. They're better than that stuff, aren't they?

LAO HEI: Sure, much better!

(*The humming continues.*)

LAO GAR: (*Leaning against the door post*) True enough, haven't I only had a few years in school? And now I'm teaching the third years, Provincial Graduates. Right, grandad?

(*Out of shot, the* TEAM LEADER *chuckles.*)

You never know in this world, you never know what people can do.

LAIDI: (*Moving into shot and giving* LAO GAR *a sudden slap on the back*) It's a deal, then, Lao Gar.

(LAO GAR *falls down.*)

LAO GAR: Hey, what do you think you're doing!

(*Out of shot, the* ZHIQING *burst out laughing.*)

EXT. PRODUCTION TEAM VILLAGE. NIGHT
Only an edge of light remains on the mountain peak, and the thatched roofs of the production team huts are indistinct. LAO HEI,

who is seeing LAO GAR *off to the edge of the village, comes to a halt.*

LAO HEI: Why not stay overnight? It might be rough going after it gets dark, you want to watch out for wild animals.

LAO GAR: Hah! I'm not scared. I've got classes first thing tomorrow. You go back now.

LAO HEI: See you!

(LAO GAR *walks off, carrying his hoe over his shoulder.*)

EXT. A PATH. NIGHT

LAO GAR *walks along with his hoe over his shoulder. Hearing a croaking noise, he turns his head, stumbles and nearly falls. He then walks faster, moving out of shot.* LAO GAR *stops suddenly to listen to something. He turns and lowers his hoe. From the dim forest, or perhaps from the grass verge, comes a jingling noise.* LAO GAR *sets his hoe on the ground and looks around. There is another rustle, from the forest, the grass or the lonely path. A white figure flashes past. Frightened,* LAO GAR *raises his hoe. There is no one on the path, but the jingling is heard again.*

LAO GAR: Who's there?

(LAO GAR *raises his hoe as if ready to strike. A laugh rings out from the desolate wild forest.*)

LAIDI: (*Out of shot*) Ha ha . . . Why are you walking so fast? You want to be first under the knife? Are you going to put down that hoe?

LAO GAR: (*In the background, putting down his hoe*) Oh, it's you. What are you doing up in the mountains this late?

(*He turns and is about to walk off.*)

LAIDI: (*Seen from behind, hastily stepping forward*) Stop!

(*Walking forward*) I wanted to ask you something, why didn't you say goodbye to your old ma before you left?

LAO GAR: We're old pals, what's the point in saying goodbye? It's not as if I'm leaving for good.

LAIDI: (*Going past* LAO GAR, *in a low voice*) Was it true what you said back there?

LAO GAR: What did I say?

(LAO GAR *stands stock still for a moment, then catches up with* LAIDI *and walks alongside.*)

LAIDI: People call you a scholar and you act like you're a genius. How can you forget something you've only just said?

LAO GAR: (*Thinking he understands*) This business about . . .

LAIDI: (*Suddenly raising her voice*) Didn't you say we'd write a song?

LAO GAR: (*Embarrassed*) Oh, that business – wasn't it you who talked about it?

LAIDI: It doesn't matter who it was . . .

LAO GAR: All right! We'll write it, and I'll get my class to sing it. It won't sound like the others, right?

LAIDI: (*Pulling at* LAO GAR) Come on, your old ma'll walk with you a bit, let's talk about it.

LAO GAR: (*Throwing off* LAIDI'*s hand*) Hey, none of this old ma business in front of your old pa, I'm older than you are!

(*He links arms with* LAIDI.)

LAIDI: Fine, my old pa can write the words and your old ma can write the music. Ha ha . . .

(LAO GAR *and* LAIDI *walk on, laughing. The dim forest. The winding path.*)

(*Out of shot*) I want to pull this off on the quiet. I'll show
Lao Hei and the others, they shouldn't think . . .
(LAIDI *and* LAO GAR *move into shot, arm in arm as before.*)
. . . that all I'm good for is cooking.
LAO GAR: OK, it's a deal. I'll let you know. I have to hurry up.
(*Pause.*) Um, do you want me to walk you back?
(LAIDI *swings her arm, shaking him off.*)
LAIDI: Who needs you!
(*With the hoe over his shoulder,* LAO GAR *slowly walks into the
distance.*)
(*Out of shot*) Lao Gar!
(LAO GAR *stops in the distance and turns round.* LAIDI *comes
running towards* LAO GAR, *so energetically that the small pieces
of mirror decorating her shoulder bag jingle. When she reaches
him she stops, takes a dictionary from her shoulder bag and
gives it to him.*)
Take it.
LAO GAR: Oh, don't you need it?
LAIDI: You take it.
(*She quickly runs back, moving out of shot. The figure of* LAO
GAR *stands far off. With his hoe over his shoulder,* LAO GAR
walks into the distance, moving out of shot.)
LAO GAR: (*Far off*) Laidi! Goodbye!
(*In the darkness it is still for a moment, then the mirrors on*
LAIDI's *shoulder bag start to jingle.*)

INT. LAO GAR'S ROOM. NIGHT
Seen from outside the window, in the lamplight, LAO GAR *is
propping up his chin with his hands, holding a pencil in one hand.
His thin arms form a triangle. He throws down the pencil, picks up
the dictionary, takes out the leaf specimen and looks at it, then
stands up. There is a clear round moon in the night sky. The moon
still shines above but it seems larger. In the background wild singing
starts up and continues for several minutes. The words are indistinct.*

One times two is two
One times three is three,
One times four is four,
Two times four is eight.
Mencius had an audience with King Hui of Liang.
The King said, 'A thousand leagues is a long way to come.'

(The dictionary lies open on the stump. In the shadow of the lamp, LAO GAR's hands turn over the pages, then pick up the dictionary. A collage of voices on the soundtrack. The lamp grows brighter, illuminating LAO GAR's thin figure. The mosquito net behind him ripples, like water or like a flag. LAO GAR sits by the side of the stump. Holding the dictionary in both hands, he lowers his head and leafs through. The singing dies away. There is a faint sound of cow bells. LAO GAR looks up. Now he hears nothing but crickets. LAO GAR lifts the lamp and walks past the north window overlooking the yard, moving out of shot. On screen we can see only the wall of split bamboo through which the light appears. The eerie sound of the door opening. LAO GAR stands in the doorway, holding a lamp. Beyond the eaves, in the shadow of the lamp, stands a white cow. LAO GAR stands under the eaves, holding the lamp, staring at it. The cow stands still, looking at LAO GAR, then turns and walks away, moving out of shot. LAO GAR stares at it.)

INT. THIRD-YEAR CLASSROOM. DARK
Seen from behind, the CHILDREN are writing, their heads lowered. LAO GAR is walking up and down the aisles between the desks.
BOY: *(Out of shot)* I can't remember how I go to school.
LAO GAR: *(Moving from right to left)* Yes, you can. You know better than anyone else what you do yourself.
(LAO GAR walks over to WANG FU. WANG FU raises his head and looks at LAO GAR.)
Finished?
(WANG FU nods and hands over his composition to LAO GAR. The other CHILDREN raise their heads to look.)
Everyone finished?
(The other CHILDREN hastily lower their heads to write. LAO GAR reads through Wang Fu's composition. On the blackboard, in large script, are the words: GOING TO SCHOOL. LAO GAR sits behind his desk, reading the compositions. In turn, the CHILDREN come forward with their compositions and return to their seats. The gong sounds noisily for the end of class.)
Class is over.

(*The* CHILDREN *rush up to the desk, looking at the compositions on the desk. More and more* CHILDREN *crowd around the desk, pressing* LAO GAR *to discuss the compositions. Close-up of the dictionary on a corner of the desk. A pair of girl's hands, very carefully, is about to pick up the dictionary.*)
(*Through the babble of voices*) I'll talk about the compositions after the break.
(*A* GIRL, *head lowered, is looking through the dictionary. After a moment she looks up and smiles in embarrassment.*)
(*Out of shot*) Go out and play!
(WANG FU *sits alone at his desk, putting his things away. In the background some* CHILDREN *are chasing each other. They dash past, shouting. Seen side on, from behind,* WANG FU *sits looking out. In the background, outside the door,* LAO GAR *is playing skipping games with the* CHILDREN. *As the rope swings, he jumps up like a monkey, making the* CHILDREN *laugh.* LAO GAR *stops playing and, passing under the eaves, walks over to* WANG FU. *The sound of the* CHILDREN *playing continues.*)

INT. THIRD-YEAR CLASSROOM. DAY
On the crossbeam in front of the classroom are carved two heads, with tongues of red paper fluttering in the breeze. Noise offscreen.
LAO GAR: (*Out of shot*) Fine! I'm going to read out two of the compositions.
(*The noise subsides.*)
(*Turning over the paper in his hands*) The topic for today is 'Going to School'. I'm going to read them aloud. The first one . . .
(*Close-up of a pair of boy's hands rolling up a twist of paper.*)
(*Out of shot*) . . . goes like this:
(*A series of drawings carved on the front of the teacher's desk: a weird sea, land and air battle scene; a teacher holding a cane and yelling 'Copy! Copy!'; a female teacher with her hair sticking out.*)
(*Out of shot*) 'Going to school, to the classroom at school, I go to the classroom at school. I walk to school.' (*With a broad grin*) That's all.
(*The* MONITOR *is dumbfounded, then giggles. Out of shot, several of the other* CHILDREN *burst out laughing. A finger*

98

with a face drawn on it pops up from a hole in one of the desks.
Another finger appears behind it.)
(*Out of shot*) Fine!
(*The fingers retract. The laughter subsides. From a straw
raincape hanging on the bamboo wall sticks out a face mask
made of cardboard.*)
(*Out of shot*) This composition is very well written. Really.
At least he used the word 'walk', that's very clear.
(*On one of the uprights in the classroom is a row of childish
footprints in red paint going up.*)
(*Out of shot*) He didn't run, he didn't fly either, and he
wasn't carried, but he walked.
(*In the background the* CHILDREN *burst out laughing.*)
GIRL: Sir, it's too short.
LAO GAR: (*Seen from behind*) It doesn't matter about being
short. In time you can write more, write clearly.
(*He puts his hand on a crossbeam.*)
BOY: (*Out of shot*) Sir, who wrote it?
LAO GAR: (*Turning his head*) You!
(*Another burst of laughter. A* BOY *rubs his nose, giggling. The
laughter continues.*)
(*Out of shot*) It's not important who wrote it.
(*Seen from behind.* LAO GAR *goes behind the teacher's desk and
turns around.*)
OK!
(*The noise subsides.*)
The second one's by Wang Fu. I'll read it out. The topic is
'Going to School'.
(*A* BOY *turns his head and looks at* WANG FU.)
'I don't have a clock at home . . .'
(*The same* BOY *turns his head round, smiling.*)
'I got up, I got dressed, I washed my face, I went to the
cookhouse to fetch breakfast, I ate breakfast . . .'
(*A* GIRL *starts smiling as she listens.*)
(*Out of shot*) I washed up my bowl . . . I picked up my
schoolbag. I don't have a clock. I walked for a long time,
there was mist in the mountains, I reached the school, I sat
down, I started class.
(*Another burst of laughter.* WANG FU, *embarrassed, raises his head.*)
Don't laugh.

(LAO GAR *moves out of shot. The cane lies on the desk. The pages of the open dictionary lift in the breeze. On the blackboard:* GOING TO SCHOOL.)

(*Out of shot*) There are too many 'I's. When you've written 'I' once, everyone understands, you don't have to keep writing it. He wrote down some facts, and what's more he noticed the mist.

GIRL: (*Out of shot*) Too many commas.

LAO GAR: (*Out of shot*) Yes, there are too many commas, all the way through. But this can be corrected. He wrote very well. Firstly, there are no wrong characters, it's clear; secondly, it's got content. What I'm asking you for now is this: firstly, the writing has to be clear. It doesn't matter if it doesn't look so nice.

(*A* GIRL *listens intently.*)

(*Out of shot*) Secondly – well, there isn't a second. Only the first. (*Seen from behind the* CHILDREN, *his hand on the crossbeam*) Secondly . . .

BOY: Sir, didn't you just say there wasn't a second?

LAO GAR: (*Smiling at himself*) Secondly, when you write compositions don't copy from newspapers. No matter what it is, don't copy. So what do you do? You think about the topic yourself, you write yourself, write what you like. It doesn't matter if you don't write much, but you must write honestly. Is this clear?

CHILDREN: (*Thunderously, banging their desks*) Yessir!

LAO GAR: Ha ha, you made me jump! It's right not might that counts!

(*The* CHILDREN *grin cheerfully.*)

INT. THIRD-YEAR CLASSROOM. DAY

Clutching their satchels, the CHILDREN *say goodbye to* LAO GAR *and go out.*

CHILDREN: (*In unison*) Good afternoon, sir!

LAO GAR: (*Out of shot*) Yes, see you all tomorrow!

(*In a moment the* CHILDREN *have disappeared.* LAO GAR *moves into shot, carrying his teaching equipment. There is a knock from the next classroom.*)

FEMALE TEACHER: (*Out of shot*) You must have been reading something weird this morning, they were laughing right through the lesson.

LAO GAR: It's good to laugh.

FEMALE TEACHER: (*Out of shot*) What did you say?

LAO GAR: I said it's good to laugh.

    (*He goes out through the door, chuckling.*)

EXT. ON THE HILLSIDE. DUSK

*The mountain range at sunset. Music. A herd of cattle ambles past.
Wearing white clothes and his face screened by a battered hat, the
COWHERD is hidden among the cattle. LAO GAR walks into shot.
The COWHERD is squatting on the ground. Head lowered, he digs at
something in the ground. LAO GAR hitches his trousers and squats
down.*

LAO GAR: Whose son are you?

    (*The COWHERD ignores him.*)

    Do you go to school?

    (*Not bothering to answer, the COWHERD goes on playing.*)

    You don't? Why not?

    (*The COWHERD lifts his face from under the hat and gazes as
    the sky for a moment, then lowers his head again.*)

    I can read, do you want me to teach you?

    (*The COWHERD squints up at him, gets up and moves out of
    shot. The sound of the COWHERD shooing the cattle. LAO GAR
    is dumbfounded, then hastily stands up. We see only two legs.
    The cattle walk off into the sunset. The COWHERD suddenly
    stops, turns his face round for a moment, then turns back and
    walks off. Looking down on the otherwise deserted hillside, we
    see LAO GAR's thin frame, his back hunched so that he is barely
    visible. The sound of the COWHERD shooing the cattle recedes.*)

EXT. LOOKING DOWN ON THE SCHOOL FROM A MOUNTAIN
SIDE. MORNING MIST

Time-lapse shot.

*The light slowly enters the western sky (seen from side on), grey and
bleary. Gradually the outline of the mountain range emerges. The
horizon gradually reddens. The clouds break up and the mist
disperses. The thatched huts, like recumbent cattle, are becoming
clearly visible. The sun climbs quickly and moves out of shot. In the*

dazzling sunlight, the school buildings become blurred. The distant sound of a wild song continues through to the first part of the next scene.

EXT. SCHOOL YARD. MORNING MIST
A dead tree in the heavy mist. A brown thatched hut and the dark red soil. A wash bowl with rippling water.

LAO GAR: (*Out of shot*) Class! You all know that the school has to repair the school roofs.

CHILDREN: (*Out of shot*) Yessir!

LAO GAR: (*Out of shot*) Our task is to cut down two hundred and thirty bamboo logs.

CHILDREN: (*Out of shot*) That many?

LAO GAR: (*Out of shot*) Tomorrow morning bring your machetes with you. We'll go up the mountain in the morning and carry them back in the afternoon.

CHILDREN: (*Out of shot*) Yessir!

MONITOR: (*Out of shot*) Sir, which team do we go to?

CHILDREN: (*Out of shot, clamouring*) Come to mine, come to mine . . .

LAO GAR: (*Out of shot*) Let's go to my old team. I'm familiar with the area, so we can start felling as soon as we get there, we won't have to look around . . .
(*The camera pans down to an empty water scoop, lying in the school yard. The CHILDREN scatter over the school yard, picking up firewood and putting it on the fire. Flames from the burning wood leap up, crackling.*)
. . . It's just that it's rather far away. But the boys can help the girls!

BOYS: Yessir! No problem.

MONITOR: We do this kind of job all the time, we're just as good as them. Who needs their help?
(*The GIRLS chorus their agreement.*)

BOY: Sir, do we have to do a composition when we get back?

LAO GAR: Let's stick to the job for now, don't worry about compositions.

BOY: I bet we have to. Mr Li always used to do it like this. Why not give us the topic now and we can write it today.

LAO GAR: Then it would certainly be copying.
(*The CHILDREN groan.*)

WANG FU: Sir, if you set the topic now I can write it today without it being copying.

LAO GAR: Wang Fu, if you drank to your parents at their wedding, then you can write today about tomorrow's bamboo felling.

(*The* CHILDREN *jeer.*)

WANG FU: OK! I'll make a bet with you.

LAO GAR: Bet what?

WANG FU: Will you really make a bet?

LAO GAR: Of course. The whole class can be the witness. OK?

CHILDREN: Yessir!

LAO GAR: Wang Fu, what's the bet?

WANG FU: You'll really make a bet?

LAO GAR: Yes. Tell me what you want.

(*The* CHILDREN *animatedly discuss which of the teacher's things he might want.*)

Why not this way: if I lose, you can have anything of mine you want. What do you want?

(WANG FU *says something in a low voice.*)

What? Ah?

(*A* BOY *standing next to* WANG FU *immediately takes off in the direction of the teachers' dorm. A moment later a crash is heard from inside* LAO GAR's *hut. Everyone stands still, gazing at the* BOY *as he runs back over. Holding the dictionary in his hand, the* BOY *halts, panting.*)

(*Out of shot*) Hand it over to the monitor. It goes to the winner tomorrow.

(*Making his way through the rest of the* CHILDREN, *the* BOY *hands the dictionary to the* MONITOR. *The* CHILDREN *stand still, looking at the dictionary as though it were a strange beast.*)

EXT. IN FRONT OF LAO GAR'S HUT. DUSK

The passageway under the eaves. Seen from behind, CHEN *is walking along the passageway, crumpling a sheet of paper in his hand.*

CHEN: Had your dinner yet?

LAO GAR: (*Out of shot*) Not yet.

CHEN: You're felling bamboo tomorrow?

(LAO GAR *is sitting on the ground, whetting his machete. He*

nods and hands over the cigarettes lying beside him.)
(*Taking a cigarette and squatting down*) How's it going?
Everything all right?

LAO GAR: All right. Oh, can you lend me your dictionary for a
bit? I'm writing something, but I've forgotten how to write
the word 'fulfil'.

CHEN: What are you writing?

LAO GAR: Song lyrics.

CHEN: Song lyrics? 'Fulfil' . . . Oh, I thought you had a
dictionary.

LAO GAR: Um, it's a bet I've made with Wang Fu. The
dictionary's with the stake-holder.

CHEN: A bet? What kind of bet?

LAO GAR: About felling bamboo.
(*Standing up*, CHEN *knocks down the gourd and hangs it up
again.*)

CHEN: So, you haven't lost your bad habits from the team. (*In
the background, his head out of shot*) If you make a bet with
the students and lose, it might not be easy to keep control
over them afterwards.

LAO GAR: (*In the foreground, whetting his machete*) What control?
They're all bright kids.

CHEN: You're not teaching according to the book, and the
higher-ups have somehow got to hear about it. As far as the
school is concerned, it doesn't matter that much, but don't
go too far.

LAO GAR: Mm.
(CHEN *goes down the hillside. After a moment, he squats down,
moving out of shot.* LAO GAR *approaches the hillside, gradually
filling the screen. He pulls a hair from his head and, facing the
setting sun, he tests the machete for sharpness.*)

EXT. RIVER SHORE. MORNING MIST
In the distance, WANG FU *comes carrying a bamboo log. He is half
naked. In the foreground, several long bamboo logs are scattered
over the river shore.* WANG FU *heaves the bamboo from his shoulder
on top of them.* WANG FU *turns and goes back into the mountain
forest shrouded in mist.*

EXT. RIVER SHORE. MORNING MIST
Through the mist, we can faintly make out a group of people in the
distance. The mountain forest in the mist. Distant sounds of wood-
chopping. Dimly visible on the shore are a fire and a solitary wooden
boat. A man wearing a straw raincape is banging the side of the
boat. WANG FU *wades through the river carrying bamboo.* LAO GAR
and the CHILDREN *approach. Apparently catching sight of* WANG
FU, *they come to a halt.* WANG FU *walks across the shore, moving*
out of shot.
WANG FU: (*Out of shot*) Sir, I've won.
    (*The sound of the* CHILDREN *giggling.*)
LAO GAR: (*Out of shot*) What?
    (WANG FU, *moving into shot, runs back to the logs, picks up*
    his jacket and runs forward.)

EXT. ON THE WAY TO FELL BAMBOO. MORNING MIST
Big trees and a bamboo fence. A path by a stream. LAO GAR *and*
the CHILDREN (*including* WANG FU) *go deep into the forest.*

EXT. ON THE WAY TO FELL BAMBOO. MORNING MIST
Amid the vegetation of a primordial forest is a huge tree forked into
three parts. LAO GAR *and the* CHILDREN *cross the stream and go*
past the huge tree.

EXT. ON THE WAY TO FELL BAMBOO. MORNING MIST
A round log forms a single-plank bridge under which the stream
flows noisily. LAO GAR *helps the* CHILDREN *to cross one by one.*

EXT. IN THE FOREST. MORNING MIST
A pile of long bamboo logs is scattered over the grass. LAO GAR *and*
the CHILDREN *approach the logs.* LAO GAR *lowers his head and*
gazes dumbly at the logs. Stripped to the waist, WANG QITONG
approaches, carrying a load of bamboo. LAO GAR *and the*
CHILDREN *gaze at him.* WANG FU *moves out of shot.* WANG
QITONG *comes closer.*
WANG FU: (*Out of shot*) Dad, Sir says he knows you.
    (*Tossing down the bamboo,* WANG QITONG *comes forward*
    with WANG FU. LAO GAR *joins them in mid-ground.*)
LAO GAR: Hello.
    (WANG QITONG *looks dumbly at* LAO GAR.)

Don't you recognize me?
(WANG QITONG *shakes his head doubtfully*.)
We loaded rice together once . . .
(WANG QITONG *still makes no response*.)
(*Smiling awkwardly*) Your son's a good student.
(WANG QITONG *nods his head and smiles at* LAO GAR. LAO
GAR *grins cheerfully. The* CHILDREN *stand around by the logs.*
WANG QITONG, LAO GAR *and* WANG FU *stand on one side*.)

WANG FU: My dad and me, we went up to the mountain to cut
bamboo before it got dark. When we'd cut down two
hundred and thirty logs, I went home and wrote my
composition. I finished it before midnight. I've left it at
home. There's a zhiqing as witness.
(WANG QITONG *sits down on the bamboo logs*.)

LAO GAR: (*Taken aback for the moment*) Good, Wang Fu.
(WANG FU *goes over to the* CHILDREN. *We see the*
CHILDREN, *also taken aback*.)

WANG FU: (*Out of shot*) You're the witness. I won the
dictionary.
(WANG FU *stands in front of the* MONITOR. LAO GAR *looks*.
WANG QITONG *gets up. The* MONITOR *takes out the
dictionary, wrapped in a yellow cloth, from her satchel.* WANG
QITONG *grins happily, waiting expectantly.* LAO GAR *is
thinking hard.* WANG FU *takes the dictionary from the*
MONITOR, *holding it in his hand*.)

LAO GAR: (*Out of shot*) Wang Fu!
(WANG FU *turns around*.)
Wang Fu, I'll give you the dictionary as a gift. You haven't
won it.
(WANG FU *raises his head, taken aback*.)
The bet we made was that you would write about today's
labour yesterday. Although you wrote your composition
yesterday, the labour was also yesterday's. The record of an
event has to come after the event. This is an
incontrovertible truth. You're an extremely serious boy and
you've done a lot for the class, and so I'm giving you the
dictionary.
(*Overcome with emotion,* WANG FU *goes towards* LAO GAR.
Taken aback, the CHILDREN *watch*.)

WANG FU: (*Out of shot*) I lost.

(LAO GAR *accepts the dictionary. The* CHILDREN *stand in silence.*)
MONITOR: Sir, give Wang Fu the dictionary!

EXT. UNDER THE EAVES. DAY
There is a chalk drawing of a house (for a hopping game) on the red earth, with faintly visible drawings of the signs for metal, wood, water, fire and earth within white squares. WANG FU *is sitting under the eaves of the teachers' dormitory, copying the dictionary.*

EXT. CLEARING. MORNING MIST
In the background the school buildings are faintly visible. WANG FU *is leaning over the stone roller, copying the dictionary. After a while, he stands up and moves his hands and feet. He takes the bottle of ink from the millstone, retreats several steps and, raising his hand, throws it into the sky.*

INT. LAO GAR'S ROOM. DUSK
Seen from outside through the window, LAO GAR *is sitting at the west window lost in thought.*

EXT. SCHOOL YARD. DUSK
Seen from behind, WANG FU *is kneeling in front of the wooden stump, copying.*

INT. LAO GAR'S ROOM. DUSK
WANG FU *is sitting at the bamboo desk, laboriously copying. The pages filled with his copying already make a pile the size of a brick.* LAO GAR, *who is sitting in front of the west window, turns and looks at* WANG FU. *He gets up, walks over to the desk and picks up the pile of papers. A sheet of brown paper is covered with entries copied very neatly from the dictionary.* WANG FU's *hand puts down the pencil and lifts the sheet of paper.*
LAO GAR: (*Taking the sheet of paper*) Wang Fu, it's time to go
    home.
    (WANG FU *looks at* LAO GAR, *shakes his head and lowers his head again to copy.* LAO GAR *puts down the paper, turns round and moves out of shot. Seen front on, from outside the window,* WANG FU *is copying in the foreground.* LAO GAR *picks up his shirt from the bed, and approaches* WANG FU *with sweets in his hand. The coloured sweets sparkle in the light of the setting sun. Bent over his copying,* WANG FU *appears not to notice.* LAO GAR *places the sweets on the desk and moves out of shot.*)
ZHIQING: (*Out of shot*) Lao Gar!

EXT. SCHOOL YARD. DUSK
Seen from behind, LAO GAR *waves and claps his hands in greeting.* LAIDI, LAO HEI *and several other* ZHIQING *come up, passing under an old hut frame. They race up to* LAO GAR. *Each is carrying various things for making food, which rattle as they go. When they reach* LAO GAR *they surround him talking and laughing warmly.*

INT. THIRD-YEAR CLASSROOM. DAY
The ZHIQING *crowd into the classroom, commenting on the shabby room. They each find themselves a desk and sit down.* LAO GAR *stands in the doorway.*

LAO HEI: Lao Gar, what are you doing standing there? Come on, give us a lesson.

LAO GAR: Who's going to say 'Stand up'?

(*Taken aback, the* ZHIQING *jeer.*)

LAIDI: I will. Stand up!

(*One by one the* ZHIQING *stand up, making a noise with the desks and benches.* LAO GAR *comes in and motions for them to sit down. The* ZHIQING *sit down, laughing.*)

LAO GAR: Quiet! Put your hands behind your backs. Anyone fooling around will catch it.

(*The* ZHIQING *protest, but put their hands behind their backs and quieten down.*)

The lesson will now begin. Today's lesson is very important, and I want you to pay attention. (*He holds up his index finger.*) First I'm going to read the text aloud. 'Once upon a time there was a mountain. On the mountain there was a temple. In the temple there was an old monk telling a story. What was the story he was telling? Once upon a time there was a mountain. On the mountain there was a temple. In the temple there was an old monk telling a story. What was the story he was telling . . .'

ZHIQING: (*Chorusing*) 'Once upon a time there was a mountain. On the mountain there was a temple. In the temple there was an old monk telling a story. What was the story he was telling? Once upon a time . . .'

(*The noise gets louder and louder as the* ZHIQING *start shouting and banging the desks. Shouting,* LAO GAR *performs the actions on a large scale. In the foreground, some* CHILDREN *are leaning on the bamboo railing in the side classroom, looking at the* ZHIQING.)

(*In the background*) What was the story he was telling? Once upon a time there was a mountain. On the mountain there was a temple. In the temple there was an old monk telling a story. What was the story he was telling . . .

(*The noise gets louder and the rhythm faster as the* ZHIQING *repeat the story. Suddenly, the shouting dies down. After a pause, there is a burst of laughter. From among the* CHILDREN *in the foreground is heard a thin, shrill* GIRL'*s voice.*)

GIRL: 'Once upon a time there was a mountain. On the mountain there was a temple . . .'

CHILDREN: (*Chorusing*) 'In the temple there was an old monk telling a story. What was the story he was telling . . .'

(*They gather up their satchels and move out of shot. The* ZHIQING *stare amazed at each other, then as one turn their heads.*)

(*Out of shot*) 'Once upon a time there was a mountain. On the mountain there was a temple. In the temple . . .'

(LAO GAR *raises his head, looking as if he is lost in thought.*)

(*In the distance*) 'Once upon a time . . .'

EXT. ON THE HILLSIDE. DUSK

CHILDREN: (*Seen from behind, going off in single file*) 'In the temple there was an old monk telling a story. What was the story he was telling . . .'

(*They go downhill, out of shot. The distant mountains in the setting sun fill the screen.*)

INT. THIRD-YEAR CLASSROOM. DUSK
LAO HEI, *his jacket over his shoulder, is sitting disconsolately on one of the classroom benches.*
LAIDI: (*Out of shot*) Lao Hei . . . Let's go!
LAO HEI: (*Sighing*) OK.
  (*He moves out of shot. On the desk is a scooped-out pomelo peel.*)

EXT. SCHOOL YARD. TWILIGHT
In the twilight, the ZHIQING *come into shot.*
LAIDI: Hey, why don't you lot go on ahead, I'm making dinner for Lao Gar.
LAO GAR: Don't get mad, but what if something happens . . .
LAIDI: (*Interrupting*) I'm going to make you a meal!
ZHIQING: OK, let's go, let's go . . .
  (LAO GAR *and* LAIDI *stand in the yard, watching them leave.*)

INT. LAO GAR'S ROOM. NIGHT
Holding up the dictionary to the light from the hut, WANG FU *stands outside leaning against the window.* LAIDI *and* LAO GAR *move into shot, passing* WANG FU. LAO GAR *moves out of shot.*
LAIDI: Ah! (*Moving out of shot*) Are you punishing your student?
LAO GAR: (*Out of shot*) Wang Fu, stop reading. Let's get the food ready.
  (WANG FU *disappears and then enters the room, going over to the desk.*)
LAIDI: (*Out of shot*) So this is Wang Fu! (*In shot*) What a hard worker! No wonder your teacher is always boasting about you. (*Seen from outside the window*) Are you doing your homework?
WANG FU: No, I'm copying the teacher's dictionary.
LAIDI: Dictionary? (*She picks up the dictionary.*) Fuck! This is my dictionary!
  (*In the background,* LAO GAR *takes off his jacket and puts it on the bed.*)
LAO GAR: Fuck! I never said it wasn't.
  (LAIDI *looks at* LAO GAR *and smiles, then turns back to* WANG FU.)
LAIDI: Do you copy this out every day?
  (WANG FU *nods.*)

Till this late?

WANG FU: It's not late.

LAIDI: No? But your team's a long way off!

WANG FU: Not so far, we always walk home.

LAIDI: (*Looking through the dictionary*) Your teacher told me
what happened about the dictionary. Look, I'll give you
the dictionary as a present.

(*She puts the dictionary on the desk.* WANG FU *turns his head
and looks at* LAO GAR, *then looks at* LAIDI, *shakes his head,
stands up and goes to the corner of the hut. He then goes to the
door carrying the basin of vegetables.* LAIDI *walks around the
desk, holding on to the chair back, and looks at* WANG FU *in
surprise.*)

LAO GAR: (*Moving into shot*) Take it, Wang Fu. She's the real
owner.

(WANG FU *is squatting in the doorway, washing the
vegetables.*)

WANG FU: (*Raising his head*) No, I'll copy. Copying makes it
stick in my mind.

LAIDI: What happens when you're finished copying?

WANG FU: When I finish school, I'll go back and work in the
team. When I finish copying I'll take it with me.
Afterwards if there's a bigger dictionary, I'll copy that out.

(LAO GAR *and* LAIDI *stand there, dumbfounded.* LAIDI *picks
up the dictionary from the desk.* WANG FU *wipes his hands and
stands up. He goes to the desk, tidies it up, picks up his satchel
and goes to the door.*)

(*To* LAO GAR) Sir, I've finished washing the vegetables. I'm
going home now.

LAO GAR: No, stay here and eat.

WANG FU: No, I'm going. (*He goes to the door, then turns round
and addresses* LAIDI.) Goodbye, ma'am.

LAIDI: (*Raising her head, in a low voice*) What did you call me?

(WANG FU *halts for a moment, turns around and goes out of
the door. After a pause,* LAIDI *moves into shot, leaning by the
side of the door.* LAIDI *stands dumbly by the door, holding the
dictionary. After a pause, she goes to the desk. Suddenly,*
LAIDI *utters an animal-like cry and hurls the dictionary on to
the pile of papers, which scatter and fall to the ground.* LAO
GAR, *moving into shot, gazes at* LAIDI. *After a pause, he*

hastily goes over and, half kneeling, half squatting, picks up the papers. LAIDI *steps back a couple of paces. The lamp flickers between them.)*

LAO GAR: Laidi, teaching like this . . . I really don't know how I should teach.

(The mirror on the wall. Seen from behind, LAIDI *moves into shot and goes up to the mirror, fixing her hair. The lamp on the tree stump.* LAO GAR *and* LAIDI *are sitting at either side of the stump, holding their bowls and eating. As* LAIDI *finishes her bowl of rice,* LAO GAR *quickly fills it up again for her.* LAIDI *takes the bowl of rice, leans forward and pushes out half into* LAO GAR'S *bowl. Suddenly, she looks at* LAO GAR *and starts giggling.* LAO GAR *lowers his head and looks at the apron around his waist. Involuntarily he also laughs, so hard that he spits out some rice.* LAO GAR *and* LAIDI *look at each other, laughing uncontrollably.)*

INT. THIRD-YEAR CLASSROOM. DAY
Seen from outside, the bamboo railing around the classroom.

LAO GAR: *(Moving along the aisle between the desks)* We've already written about many things, things that we know from our own experience. Today, I want you to write about a person you know. People are living beings, it's not easy to write about them. Anyway, give it a go. See if you can add a bit to what you did before.

BOY: Sir, I want to write about our team cook.

LAO GAR: All right.

GIRL: Sir, I'll write about the driver.

LAO GAR: Do you know him well? As long as you do, it's all right.

MONITOR: *(Standing up)* Sir, I'll write about you.

LAO GAR: Me? Ha ha. I've only been here a few months, do you know me well enough? Do you know whether I snore at night?

(The CHILDREN *laugh.)*

It's all right, go ahead.

(Going in front of the teacher's desk, LAO GAR *mutters to himself for a minute.)*

Oh, I want you to stay behind a bit after class, there's a
good song I want to teach you.
(*The* CHILDREN *agree cheerfully.*)

EXT. SCHOOL YARD. DAY
Seen from inside the classroom. LAO GAR *leans against the door
looking at a piece of paper in his hand. In the background,* CHEN
comes out of the office, takes a couple of steps then turns back.
COMRADE WU *comes out of the office and says something to* CHEN.
CHEN *comes forward again and is about to go over to the classroom
when he stops again and whispers to* COMRADE WU. *After a
moment,* CHEN *finally turns round and comes forward.* CHEN *goes to
the door of the third-year classroom and says something to* LAO GAR,
*who is leaning against the door. Then he turns and takes a few steps
away, then goes back to whisper something, then walks away again.*
LAO GAR *follows* CHEN *towards the office.*

INT. SCHOOL OFFICE. DAY
COMRADE WU *sits at the desk under the skylight, smoking.*
CHEN: (*Coming through the door*) Here we are.
    (*He picks up the thermos and pours some water.* LAO GAR
    enters through the door.)
    Er, this is Comrade Wu from the head office, he's got
    something to say to you.
    (LAO GAR *nods and squats down by the door in the foreground.*
    COMRADE WU *takes off his cap, exposing his bald head. He
    lifts his head and looks at the skylight, squinting at the glare.*
    CHEN, *noticing, goes over, picks up a stick and hurries outside.*)
WU: I hear you've been betting with the students.
    (LAO GAR *nods his head.*)
    What lesson are you up to now?
    (CHEN *returns with the stick. He stands in the middle of the
    room, not knowing how to use it.*)
LAO GAR: I'm still teaching, but I'm not using the textbook.
WU: Why not?
LAO GAR: (*Pauses.*) It's useless.
    (*Taking the cigarette that* CHEN *hands over,* WU *offers it to*
    LAO GAR.)
WU: Cigarette?

LAO GAR: I don't smoke. (*He gets up.*) Thanks.
  (*There is a bang as the skylight hatch falls, and inside the room
  it immediately gets dark.* LAO GAR, CHEN *and* COMRADE WU
  raise their heads to look, laughing hollowly.)

EXT. SCHOOL YARD. DAY
In the background, a pig wanders around. LAO GAR *comes out of
the office and wanders over.*

INT. THIRD-YEAR CLASSROOM. DAY
Seen front on, the CHILDREN *are talking among themselves in low
voices. They look expectantly to the left.*

EXT. SCHOOL YARD. DAY
LAO GAR *is about to go into the classroom. A basketball sails out
slowly from behind the tree stump.*

INT. THIRD-YEAR CLASSROOM. DAY

The CHILDREN *are seen front on.*

LAO GAR: (*Out of shot*) Everyone finished?

GIRL: (*Standing up and pointing a finger*) Sir!

(*On the desk is a neat pile of papers.* LAO GAR *picks up the papers, looks through a few, pauses for a moment at one, and lifts his head.*)

LAO GAR: Good. Wang Fu, come and read out your composition. Come on!

(WANG FU *gets up and goes to the desk, takes the paper and goes back to his seat. A* BOY *picks up a bench and places it behind the teacher's desk.* WANG FU *holds his composition. Inside the classroom it is very quiet. The* CHILDREN *turn their heads to look at* WANG FU. LAO GAR, *seen from behind, sits leaning against his desk.*)

WANG FU: 'My Father.' My father is the strongest man in the world. No one in our team can beat him when it comes to carrying loads. My father eats more than anyone else in the world. My mother always lets him eat all the food we have. This is right, because my father has to work, and his wages support our whole family. But my father says he is not as strong as Wang Fu, because Wang Fu can read and write. My father is a mute, but I know what he means. Therefore, I want to study and learn how to speak for him. My father is very hard working. He was sick today, but later on he got out of bed. He still wanted to go to work so he wouldn't lose a day's pay. I have to go to school so I can't stand in for him now. In the white morning sunlight, my father went up the mountain. He walked into the white sunshine. I think my father has got his strength back.

(WANG FU *goes up to the front, gives the composition back to* LAO GAR, *turns round and goes back. The sound of wild singing is heard.* WANG FU *halts and turns his head round.* LAO GAR, *seen from behind, gets up, his hair sticking up like a bush.* WANG FU *looks at him.*)

LAO GAR: (*Standing in front of the blackboard*) You may remember during one lesson, I wrote up a word on the blackboard. Wang Fu underlined it and then I rubbed it out. It was a word that I made up. (*Pauses.*) Back at the team, I used to graze the cows. Cows are very stubborn

creatures. You can beat them and curse them, but they just
blink at you and go on eating what they want. Sometimes
they go wild. That's when I pee.
(*One* CHILD *laughs. The others shush him.*)
Cows love salty things, and pee is salty. Usually they can't
get it. Sometimes I'd hold myself in and wait until we got
up the mountain before I'd take a pee . . . that day, I saw a
cowherd peeing for his cattle . . .
(LAO GAR *turns around, writes the word 'Cattle' on the
blackboard, and then adds the word 'Water' underneath it,*

117

forming his invented, composite character for 'Cattlepiss'. Then he turns around and smiles. Seen from behind, the CHILDREN *sit upright.*)

EXT. THE OLD HUT FRAME. DUSK
The CHILDREN, *seen from behind, are sitting by the old hut frame.*
LAO GAR: (*Clapping his hands*) OK! The girls need a bit more practice. Let's take it slowly.
(*The* MONITOR *gives the note and the* GIRLS *begin singing. After the first two lines, the* BOYS *gradually join in.*)
CHILDREN: (*Singing*)
> One two three four five,
> The third-year class has really tried.
> Now they've learned to read and write,
> When they leave school, their future's bright.

(*Suspended over the hut frame in the mist is a bamboo pole. A* BOY *goes over and pokes it. The pole starts swinging like a perpetual-motion machine, as if beating time.*)
> Five four three two one,
> The third-year class is second to none.
> Each pair of shoulders supports one head,
> They write what they think, not what they've read.

(*The* CHILDREN *repeat the song slowly,* LAO GAR *waving his hands to beat time.*)

INT. THIRD-YEAR CLASSROOM. DUSK
LAO GAR *sits behind his desk, looking at the compositions in his hand.* CHEN *sits in one of the students' places opposite him, smoking. The distant sound of the* CHILDREN *leaving.* CHEN *fidgets with a piece of chalk.*
LAO GAR: (*Out of shot*) I'd like to keep the students' last compositions, would that be any problem?
CHEN: (*Shakes his head, then nods his head.*) It's right not to have made a scene. If you had . . .
(LAO GAR *gives a faint smile.*)
Do you think it's not right?
LAO GAR: (*Muttering to himself*) No, it's right!
CHEN: (*Seen from behind*) We're going to burn off soon. Burning off's a fine sight.

LAO GAR: (*Standing with his hands on the crossbeam*) I've been here seven years, I don't remember how many times I've made fires up in the mountains.
(*Smiling, he goes to the left, hops over the bamboo railing and leans against the wall.*)

INT. LAO GAR'S ROOM. DARK
The open window. LAO GAR *enters, pulls down the bamboo blind and moves out of shot. The densely woven bamboo blind fills the screen, only a few rays of sunlight penetrating between the cracks.* LAO GAR *shoulders his satchel and moves out of shot.* LAO GAR *stands by the door, looks around the room, goes out and shuts the door. The dictionary is lying on the tree stump, and underneath is a pile of papers as high as a brick. On the lower half of the tree stump is written in chalk:* WANG FU, FROM NOW ON DON'T COPY ANYTHING, DON'T EVEN COPY THE DICTIONARY. *The growth rings on the tree stump shine in the soft light.*

EXT. LOOKING DOWN ON THE SCHOOL FROM A MOUNTAINSIDE. MORNING MIST
A heavy mist covers the school: it is misty, still and damp. LAO GAR, *carrying his bags over his shoulder, walks along the red soil-path.*

EXT. THE HILLSIDE BESIDE THE STONE ROLLER. MORNING MIST
LAO GAR *walks up to the stone roller, treading on the wooden frame, and walks downhill.*

EXT. MOUNTAIN SLOPE. MORNING
A band of light falls in a slight depression as the mist breaks to reveal a white sun. Seen from behind, LAO GAR *walks on.*

EXT. EASTER ISLAND. MORNING MIST
On a slight incline, the screen is filled with tree trunks of different shapes and sizes. A white mist covers the trunks, which are only dimly visible. There is an atmosphere of mystery, as on an Easter Island. Seen from behind, LAO GAR *walks into shot. When he reaches the tree trunks, he comes to a dead stop. Seen from behind,* LAO GAR *walks around the trunks. Seen from front on,* LAO GAR

seems to hear something. Seen from behind, LAO GAR *turns his head round. Seen from front on,* LAO GAR's *gaze wanders, following the noise. The* COWHERD *is standing under a large tree trunk shaped like a boot, peeing. Close-up of the* COWHERD, *his face covered by his battered hat, as he slowly raises his head. Seen from side on,* LAO GAR *and the* COWHERD *stand among the tree trunks facing each other.* LAO GAR *looks around, pleased but also puzzled. One tree trunk resembles a dragon. One tree trunk resembles a T'ang court attendant. A straw hat hangs on a tree trunk, swaying, just like a human figure.* LAO GAR *gazes around, unable to take it all in. A tree trunk shaped like a penis. A tree trunk shaped like a platypus. A tree trunk like a man with both arms outstretched as if to embrace the earth. The tree trunk 'wearing' the straw hat.* LAO GAR's *gaze travels round. Sounds well up on the soundtrack, then fade down. A tree trunk shaped like an ostrich. A tree trunk bound with creepers. A withered tree trunk shaped like a cactus. A tree trunk like a human figure. The tree trunk with the straw hat. There*

is no sign of the COWHERD in front of the tree shaped like a boot. *Seen from behind,* LAO GAR *turns his head around, searching for the* COWHERD. *A close-up of the* COWHERD *turning his head. The* COWHERD *walks down the distant mountain slope, gradually diminishing to a black dot.* LAO GAR *stands stock still among the blackened tree trunks. A smile appears on* LAO GAR'*s face. Slowly he unbuttons his collar.*

EXT. LOOKING DOWN ON THE SCHOOL FROM A
MOUNTAINSIDE. DUSK
Smoke rises from the whole mountainside: they are burning off. The school is only intermittently visible through the smoke. Various sounds intermingle: children playing, cheering, cowbells, explosions from excavations in the mountains, tree felling, trees crashing to the ground, whistling and the ZHIQING *chanting a circular story, getting louder and louder and louder. The sound continues to the end of the scene. The flames rise. Fierce flames and thick smoke mask the school. The fire continues to rage, the smoke is undiminished. The fire gradually dies down, the smoke disperses. The smoke and flames gradually die away. Only the silent embers and last wisps of smoke remain.*

INT. THIRD-YEAR CLASSROOM. DUSK
The invented character for 'Cattlepiss' is on the blackboard.

EXT. MOUNTAINSIDE TWILIGHT
The upper half of the setting sun hangs over the mountain range.

INT. THIRD-YEAR CLASSROOM. DUSK
The empty classroom. The end title appears superimposed in the bottom right corner of the frame.